Match Racing

Other titles of interest

The Yacht Racing Rules: A Complete Guide Mary Pera
The complete rules together with explanations of their
interpretation and meaning. Full use is made of international and
national case law, and illustrations clarify difficult race situations.
Mary Pera is chairman of the Royal Yachting Association
racing rules committee and a leading member of the committee of
the IYRU.

Paul Elvström Explains the Yacht Racing Rules
Paul Elvström
This book covers every tricky situation likely to be met in a race.
Two-colour line drawings and cross referencing assist the reader
throughout, and each book carries the familiar set of plastic
boats with buoys and a wind arrow to help analyse protests.

The Rules Book Eric Twiname, revised by Bryan Willis
This book assumes a race situation and then looks at which rule
applies, so the reader works his way round the course from the
start to the windward mark, offwind legs, to the finish, studying
all the situations that can arise. It is thus truly the helmsman's
view of the yacht racing rules.

Championship Tactics
Gary Jobson, Tom Whidden and Adam Loory
The tactical manual for the racing sailor. It contains lessons from
decades of world-class competition and melds expert advice and
professional secrets with a rich collection of anecdotes from the
greatest races of our time.

Race Winner!: A Cockpit Guide to Faster Sailing
Ian and Richard Nicolson
This unique book, used like the pilot's cockpit check, is intended
to be used before, during and after a race to pinpoint, analyse
and rectify mistakes. For dinghies, cruiser and ocean racers, for
novice and expert alike, this book can instantly help a crew
improve their position through the fleet to first place. Clear
instructions advise on essential sail and rigging adjustments for
the wind direction and speed. This is a book no serious racing
sailor can afford to be without.

Match Racing

The tactics and rules of match race sailing
for competitors, umpires, judges, and race committees

Bryan Willis and John Doerr

Based on the International Yacht Racing Rules 1993-96
including Appendix B6, Match Racing and the
IYRU umpires' call book

ADLARD COLES NAUTICAL
London

Criticisms, advice and ideas for
new tactical scenarios from readers
are warmly welcomed; please send
to the authors c/o the publishers.

First published 1993 by Adlard Coles Nautical
an imprint of A & C Black (Publishers) Ltd
35 Bedford Row, London WC1R 4JH

Copyright © Bryan Willis and John Doerr 1993

First edition 1993

ISBN 0 7136 3454 5

A CIP catalogue record for this book is available from the
British Library.

Typeset in Sabon by Keepdate Publishing, Newcastle upon Tyne
Printed and bound in Great Britain by
Butler and Tanner Ltd, Frome and London

Contents

Foreword
by Peter Gilmour

Throughout the last century the yacht racing rules have been developed and defined to keep yachts apart whilst racing. Now, with sailing being characterised by two disciplines – that of match racing and fleet racing – the former has created a whole new set of challenges for rule makers, judges and sailors. *Match Racing*, written by Bryan Willis and John Doerr, superbly sets the stage as we head towards the 21st century.

With the winning of the America's Cup in 1983 by Australia II, breaking sport's longest winning streak in history, and the subsequent Australian defence that followed in 1987, an unprecedented awareness of match racing was created. I had the opportunity with the *Kookaburra* campaign as a defender to be taught by Bryan Willis the intricacies and complexities of using the yacht racing rules to manipulate an opponent in a match race; this style became the norm rather than the exception.

Quite clearly the principle of protesting several times in a race was not contemplated by regatta organisers, as results were often not known until the next day. To resolve this, a system of umpiring was created. Both Bryan and John were instrumental in developing and improving this system, now known as Appendix B6.

Sailors, umpires and race organisers are so satisfied with the system that it was confidently used throughout the 1992 America's Cup and the Olympic Games. Whether it is for top level racing or a club winter series, the use of umpiring and Appendix B6 for match racing really is ideal.

To understand the rules, the principles, the case histories, how an advantage can be gained and be able to learn more about the sport, *Match Racing* is a very in-depth and accurate analysis for the competitive sailor.

Bryan and John, having participated as international judges, umpires and rules advisers and also enjoyed active racing, have prepared an excellent, up to date publication that will serve as the key manual for a successful part of every racing sailor's inventory.

Foreword
by Goran Petersson, Chairman IYRU Racing Rules Committee

Never in my wildest dreams could I have imagined the consequences of the Maxi owner's request of the judges at the Maxi World Match Racing Championships in Newport in June 1987. They asked that a judging system be implemented on the following day; this would free them to enjoy their evenings rather than attending protest hearings after the races. The judges achieved this goal and they came up with an umpiring system that was used for the following days of racing. Since then, match racing as well as umpiring has developed fast and become popular all over the world.

Competitors have improved their match racing skills and tactics. As a result umpires have had to produce rule interpretations and a working system that meets the new demands for immediate and correct decisions arising from the incidents on the water, that develop so quickly.

We now have a system of umpiring that works well for match race sailing events. The yacht racing rules, originally designed to avoid collisions between yachts, are now being used to try to gain tactical advantage over the other competitor. This fundamental change of the use of the rules has led to many new tactics and manoeuvres that were not anticipated by the rule makers. A most thorough understanding and knowledge of the racing rules has now become even more necessary in order to be able to act as a good umpire.

The authors' passion for and ability to analyse this development in match racing, including unlimited hours of umpiring, discussing tactics and rule interpretations with the competitors, combined with their own exceptional practical experience over many years, made them decide to work together on this book.

The result is that Willis and Doerr have produced an indispensable tool for anyone interested or involved in the lastest developments in the sport of match racing. This book is a comprehensive guide for competitors, umpires, judges and race committees alike. It is at the same time an explanation and discussion of the rules and methods of organising, conducting and judging match races at the highest level.

Match racing today involves an extraordinary variety of manoeuvres and tactics - ones that were not foreseen even four years ago. It is this tremendous scope that makes match racing so interesting - and writing a comprehensive book about it so complicated.

I'm sure *Match Racing* will contribute immensely to the continued enjoyment of match race sailing and umpiring. The authors should be congratulated upon this evidence of their devotion to match racing and be thanked for their contribution to this sport.

Acknowledgements

Match racing events have attracted media coverage and resulting sponsorship, but a significant contribution to the rapid growth in popularity of the sport during the past few years, has been that competitors, yacht racing judges and race organisers have worked together in a remarkable spirit of co-operation to strive to perfect the system of umpiring. It has been great fun to work with many international judges and umpires and the world's best skippers to develop this popular way of judging disputes during a race, the success of which has had such a dramatic effect on everyone's enjoyment of match racing. Many of these judges and skippers have contributed valuable information and viewpoints for this book.

In particular we'd like to thank Peter Gilmour, one of the world's most successful and respected sailors, who has not only enjoyed many great successes as a skipper, but has contributed with selfless energy and dedication to promoting the sport and helping organisers and fellow sailors. Bryan had a lot of fun working with Peter and also with Iain Murray, another great sailor with many skills, in the defence of the America's Cup in 1986-7 in Fremantle. Peter was instrumental in establishing and developing the International Sailors Association, and is currently its President. There are other top-ranking match racing skippers who have also contributed much time and thought. In particular we'd like to thank Russell Coutts, Eddie Warden-Owen, Peter Isler and Rod Davis, all of whom have made significant contibutions to the development of match racing.

Of the International Judges we must thank Goran Petersson, chairman of the IYRU Racing Rules Committee, with whom we have spent many happy hours in numerous locations throughout the world, judging and umpiring match races and discussing every conceivable tactical scenario. The Twelve Metre Championship in the mid summer of 1988, in Lulea near the Arctic Circle, was typical of some of the great times working together. Races were sailed on the flat warm water between the islands, in constant daylight, one race *started* at midnight! Just months earlier, cars had *driven* round the course (on thick ice) to see where the marks might be laid.

It was Tom Ehman who brought the idea of judging on-the-water to the IYRU conference in November 1987. His enthusiasm has continued since then, and he has taken a leading role in its development. He persuaded the America's Cup representatives to agree to this form of judging for the America's Cup. There is no doubt that the explosive popularity of match racing owes much to the introduction of umpiring. Early in 1988 the Royal Lymington Yacht Club, and in particular Eileen Caulcutt, Nick Ryley and Tony Blachford, committed the Royal Lymington Cup to using umpires, backing this commitment with trials in the Solent. This provided both of us with our first hands-on experience. Goran, Tom and Bryan developed many of the basic ideas for umpiring at the spectacular America's Cup re-match between Iain Murray and the irrepressible Dennis Conner in the *Kookaburras* in Sydney Harbour in January 1989.

Graeme Owens from Perth, Australia has spent countless hours studying procedures and sailing instructions, in addition to umpiring more events than anyone else in the world. His contribution has been very significant indeed.

Cy Gillette from Hawaii has a lifetime of yacht racing experience and, althouth he is well into his seventies and has had both hips replaced, is still ready and able to bounce around the ocean in an umpires' boat, *and* bring a clear mind to a jury meeting afterwards. He is certainly a great man.

Mary Pera has given both of us much wise advice over many years. Regrettably, her exceptional mental abilities are no longer matched by physical good health and she has not been able to join in the fun on-the-water.

Freddie Ehström from Helsinki provided the schedule of rule changes, and many other judges and umpires have helped and contributed freely to the development of this new branch of the sport, including Paul Bennett, Bill Bensten, Trygve Bernhardsen, Joe Butterfield, Graeme Hayward, Tony Mooney, Kaoru Ogami, John Ripard, Ralph Roberts, Bertie de Speville and Hal Wagstaff.

John's racing skipper, Tony Blachford, went through the manuscript with great diligence and made many suggestions for improvement, and the long suffering Sonia Mayes has never ceased to give us encouragement and good advice.

To all these, our friends, "thank you".

Lastly and perhaps most important of all, thanks must go to our children - Tammi, Jay, Pip and Kim, (Bryan's), and Alex and Katie (John's) - for allowing us both the time to attend all the events throughout the world and to spend many hours writing this book.

Bryan Willis
John Doerr
1992

Introduction

The main fascination of yacht racing as a sport is that it is infinitely complex and therefore impossible to master; few yachts have ever sailed a perfect race, or sailed the course in the fastest possible time. Success often comes by making fewer errors than anyone else, in situations where there is a myriad of variables never again to be exactly repeated.

Match racing, that special branch of the sport of yacht racing in which just two yachts compete, adds another dimension by requiring successful skippers not only to have the ability to squeeze the last ounce of speed from their vessels when necessary, but also to be able to outmanoeuvre their opponent in boat to boat battles.

This book is primarily for sailors competing in match races and for umpires judging match races. The aim is to explain how the game is played, and many of the tactics that can be employed to gain control and hence win the match.

The term 'match race' may seem contradictory. In tennis, boxing, golf, darts and football a person, partnership or team competes directly against another person, partnership or team; the interaction between the two sides is fundamental to the game. Those are 'matches'.

In a 'race' on the other hand, a person or team tries to complete a course in less time than another or, more usually, many others. A sailing 'match race' is truly a mix of both since there *is* a course and whoever crosses the finishing line first is indeed the winner, but the winner might not have completed the course in the fastest time, or even achieved a better average speed. This is because one boat is often forced by her rival to cross the starting line prematurely or many seconds after the starting signal, and the two will sail different tracks around the course. Interaction between the two yachts begins several minutes before the start as each tries to be in an advantaged position at the moment of the starting signal. If they are evenly matched, the interacting will continue around the course.

While on the subject of terms, let's cover the use of the words 'yacht' and 'yacht racing'. Match racing is best sailed in identical boats. They could be anything from Maxis 82 ft (25m) long, weighing 29 tons (30,000 kg) with a crew of twenty three to Optimist dinghies (which are often lighter than their skipper), or sailboards, or multihulls, or even radio controlled models. The common term for all of these is 'yacht' and the sport of racing sailing boats is universally known as 'yacht racing'. The size of the yachts is immaterial, since the basic rules are the same for all yachts. However, throughout the book (and especially relevant in the sections on tactics) the use of reasonably heavy displacement yachts is assumed, as favoured by the organisers of major international regattas. It should be appreciated that some of the manoeuvres described are not possible in dinghies or other light displacement craft which, because of their ability to manoeuvre easily, are not so suitable for match racing. There is no reason why they should not be used but the game would be more of a speed race between two yachts rather than a tactical battle.

Match racing is as different from fleet racing as boxing is from a running race. Although the same rules that are used for fleet racing, with some important exceptions, apply equally to match racing, certain manoeuvres and practices that are acceptable in match racing would be considered unsporting and sometimes dangerous in fleet racing. Close manoeuvring, with the intention of controlling the other yacht and encouraging or forcing her to make an error and infringe a rule, are a common and accepted part of the game of match racing. Such actions could be an infringement of the fundamental 'fair sailing' rule and could be penalised heavily were it to be practised in fleet racing without good reason. (Such practices would, however, be acceptable in fleet racing by a competitor needing to control a particular rival to protect an overall position near the end of a series.) Not every yacht racing enthusiast will like match racing - it is certainly an aggressive sport.

Another major difference is the way in which rule 35, Limitations on Altering Course, applies. Although the rule is interpreted in exactly the same way for both branches of the sport, in fleet racing at a crowded start a right of way yacht altering course must give the opportunity for a give way yacht to manoeuvre to keep clear, having taken into account all the other yachts in the vicinity. In match racing, however, the give way yacht is expected to respond immediately to the manoeuvre of her sole rival. This difference means that in match racing there is much close manoeuvring, making the game more exciting both for players and spectators. Should the racing rules be interpreted in such a way that close manoeuvring and the controlling of one yacht by another be prohibited, match racing would simply become a race between two yachts.

Match racing can provide the opportunity for exciting television programmes and, although match races comprise a tiny proportion of races sailed, the majority of TV coverage is, and doubtless will continue to be, of match racing. Exciting media coverage attracts sponsors and the money from sponsors funds some spectacular events.

The most prestigious match race is without doubt the America's Cup, which has always been as much a competition in yacht design as a match race series. The first challenge in 1870 was in a schooner (the fastest vessels of the day), but the ten events from 1958 to 1987 were sailed in Twelve Metre formula yachts. In 1992 a new class was introduced, the International America's Cup Class, which is, as were the Twelve Metres, a development class. That is, a designer has considerable scope within certain parameters. A formula using measurements of sail area, length and displacement must result in an answer not exceeding 42 metres. However, inevitably the fastest boats for any given wind and wave conditions all have many similarities. To gain a significant boat-speed advantage something which is conceptually new is required. In 1983 it was Ben Lexcen's wing keel which resulted in Alan Bond's 'Australia II' winning the America's Cup from the New York Yacht Club, which had successfully defended it many times over a period of 132 years.

The America's Cup went through troubled times in the three years following San Diego Yacht Club's successful recapture of the Cup from the Royal Perth Yacht Club in 1987. The monohull challenge by Mercury Bay Yacht Club of New Zealand and the successful, though disputed, defence by San Diego's multihull and the ensuing lengthy court battles resulted in the interest of some of the world's best skippers, crews and event organisers turning to another form of match racing event whereby a number of experienced clubs invite well known skippers to compete against each other in identical yachts. The first club to organise such an event was the Long Beach Yacht Club in California, with its Congressional Cup in 1967. In 1977 the Royal Lymington Yacht Club followed suit, and by 1988 France, Australia, New Zealand, Japan, Hong Kong, Bermuda, Yugoslavia and USA East Coast each had a club running an annual international event, some with big prize money, and most with extensive TV coverage attracting generous sponsorship. The clubs formed the World Match Racing Conference to promote the sport of match racing, and the first World Championship was held in Fremantle during 1988. The sailors formed the 'World Match Race Sailors' Association' (now the International Sailors' Association) and formulated a ranking system similar to that used for international golf. In 1989 the International Yacht Racing Union created its Match Racing Committee and took over the running of the ranking system.

Interest in match racing in identical boats continues to grow, and many clubs throughout the world are now organising match racing competitions: club 'ladders', interclub challenges and professional international invitation regattas. The 1992 Olympics included match racing for the first time to decide the medal winners in the Soling class, and the IYRU has originated a high profile match racing championship in which member nations compete for the Nations Cup.

In its simplest form, the organisation needed to run a match race is negligible. Given two similar or, better still, identical yachts, the skippers can agree on a starting system, a course, and run their own match, with no race committee, no signals and no umpires. However, at major events where there is a need for an efficient race committee, judges, umpires, spectator control, scorers, provisions for the media and so on, the number of support vessels and personnel far outnumber the skippers and crews.

At major international competitions many events were, up to 1987, spoiled by the numerous protests by lodged yachts against their opponents which, in the traditional manner, were resolved during long evenings in the jury room, often overturning the on-the-water results.

A major break-through in the development of the sport of match racing was the introduction of on-the-water judging or 'umpiring' as it is now officially known. Two judges in a fast motorboat manoeuvre close to the competing yachts. In response to a claim by a yacht that a rule has been infringed they may impose an immediate penalty (such as a turn) which will disadvantage the infringer but will not necessarily determine the result of the match. In developing the rules and procedures for umpiring, the opportunity was seized to transfer from the yachts to the umpires the right to judge peripheral matters, like hitting marks, to free the game from the problem of protests.

Competitors' attitudes need to be different when umpires are judging on-the-water; nothing is to be gained from remembering the detail of an incident as one needs to do when there is to be a conventional post race hearing, nor from arguing with the umpires. Experienced match racing skippers know that they will not always agree with the decisions, and of course some decisions will be wrong; however, the best policy for a skipper is to take a penalty promptly when signalled by the umpires, then forget about the incident and get on with the match.

Another difference in attitude is the need to be reluctant to become involved in complex tactical scenarios which might not be appreciated by the umpires judging the match, since there will be no opportunity to explain it to them. The introduction of umpiring has changed the way the game is played and made it a better game: more enjoyable for the skippers and crews, also for the umpires, judges, organisers and spectators.

During the 1987 America's Cup defence series, Bryan was rules advisor to the successful Kookaburra syndicate. With the enthusiastic support of tactician Derek Clark, 'starting helmsman' Peter Gilmour and skipper Iain Murray, interaction tactics were used that encouraged the opposition to infringe a rule and often resulted in contact; thus the outcome of the race often became immaterial as the ensuing protest would determine the winner. Who would not luff hard to cause contact when in a leeward yacht, with luffing rights, being overhauled to windward by ones rival for a major championship? Complex scenarios and tactics were developed and employed, but often had to be explained and irrefutable evidence produced, in the jury room. With umpiring, which of course we both support wholeheartedly, complex manoeuvres may be lost on even the most astute umpires, and therefore have become inappropriate.

Notation

Describing yacht racing scenarios and even just talking about two yachts racing can be confusing. It is easier to follow if the boats can be clearly identified. We have chosen to designate our yachts Blue and Yellow as these are the colours of the flags most commonly used to identify the yachts in international match racing.

In the figures Blue is always shaded while Yellow remains clear. Numbers are used to show the progress of our yachts during a scenario.

I
The principles

The game

The basic game of match race sailing consists of two yachts each with the objective of crossing the finishing line before her opponent while complying with the racing rules (and sailing instructions, etc). A yacht is usually permitted to manoeuvre against her opponent to protect or enhance her own position, prevent her opponent from passing, or take advantage of a situation by forcing her opponent to infringe a rule so that her opponent is penalised or disqualified.

Provided that those on board a yacht do not do anything dishonourable, then what counts is what the yacht actually does, and sometimes what hails (and the accompanying hand signals when umpiring is used) are made. Intentions are usually irrelevant.

As with the rules of other sports, the yacht racing rules are generally framed to give advantage to whoever is in the lead. Each yacht's objective is simple: to be the first to cross the finishing line with no outstanding penalties, having started correctly, sailed the course, and complied with any special requirements. The simplest way to achieve this is to be in an advantageous, controlling position at the start and to remain ahead and in control for the entire race. With evenly matched boats and crews, a good start usually results in winning the match, although the new tendency for downwind finishes means that a small lead is not always sufficient to ensure victory.

With some exceptions, only when the two yachts are on a collision course does the give way yacht become obliged to take evasive action. There is usually, but not always, no obligation on a give way yacht to anticipate that the right of way yacht will alter course on to a collision course. (An example of an exception to this principle is when a port tack, close hauled yacht approaches a windward mark as her opponent, on starboard tack, is rounding the mark and assuming a proper course.)

Frequently one of the two yachts is in a controlling position. During the race on upwind legs the yacht in control is either ahead and in such a position that any windshift will not benefit the other yacht, or close ahead in a position where her dirty wind or backwind is adversely affecting her opponent, or her opponent is trapped and unable to tack because of the proximity of the controlling yacht. On downwind legs, protecting a lead is often difficult and, unless well ahead, the leader will be concerned with ensuring he is inside or ahead at the next mark rather than being 'in control'.

In the pre-start period it is usually the yacht astern that is in control, preventing the yacht ahead from manoeuvring as she would wish. However, the initiative is frequently with the yacht being controlled: what she does will determine the reaction of the controlling yacht.

The two parts of a match race

There are two distinct parts to a match race: the pre-start period and the race itself.

In the pre-start period there is no 'proper course', which is significant from the point of view of the rules. The two yachts manoeuvre against each other with two objectives: to encourage the other to infringe a rule so that she will have to take a penalty after the starting signal, but, if that is not achieved, to be in a controlling position at the start or to get a significant advantage at the start. Being 'in control' at the start doesn't necessarily mean being in the lead at the moment of the starting signal; the object is to be 'in control' soon after the start. With superior speed and timing it is possible to be second across the starting line, but achieve a controlling position very soon after. Depending upon the experience and confidence of the skippers and crews, there is often a psychological advantage to be gained by the skipper who is clearly in control during the pre-start period.

During the race itself the leader tries to protect and extend her lead and the losing yacht tries to overtake.

Protesting

A part of the game of match racing is to encourage or force one's opponent to infringe a racing rule. When umpiring is used a yacht that infringes a racing rule is not expected to take the appropriate penalty until she is penalised by the umpires, and in most situations the umpires may not penalise a yacht unless the other yacht protests.

In the game of cricket the same principle becomes a farce at times, since the team fielding will shout 'howzthat?' whenever there is the slightest chance that the batsman might be ruled by the umpires as 'out'. In match racing, a yacht that protests without a genuine claim that an opponent has infringed is herself at risk of penalty.

When umpiring is used (which is now so common in match racing that its use is assumed throughout the book unless specified otherwise) a protest claiming an infringement for which an immediate penalty would be appropriate is signalled by the display of international code flag Y; for other claims of an infringement, and when there are no umpires, flag B is displayed.

Seeking redress

A 'request for redress' is a claim by a yacht that has lost a match through no fault of her own as a result of an 'action or omission of the race committee' (or because of some other, but much less common permitted reason). The Match Racing Appendix B6 requires that a yacht requesting redress displays code flag B at the first reasonable opportunity after she becomes aware of the circumstances justifying her request, but not later than 5 minutes after finishing. The umpires will approach the yacht soon after she crosses the finishing line to discover what the problem is. Should the yacht in question win the match, she would not need to proceed with this request.

The rules of the game

Every game has rules that define it. The rules defining the game of match racing are the International Yacht Racing Rules (IYRR), including amendments and additions in Appendix B6 (Match Racing), plus the sailing instructions written by the club organising the event, and the class rules or 'rules for inspection' which describe what is and is not permitted to be done to the yachts being used. It has to be said that there are also some unwritten laws of what is acceptable practice in the game.

The IYRR are fixed for four year periods in the November following each Olympics, but the match racing appendix (like other appendices) can be changed each November. A specialist appendix (then 4B) for match racing was first decided in November 1988 (and published in January 1989) and was changed in 1989, 1990, 1991 and again in 1992. With the publication of the 1993-96 rules the appendix was again modified and became Appendix B6. It is now hoped that a period of stability will be achieved with the 1993-96 rule book but every match racing sailor, umpire and race official should be in possession of a current Appendix B6.

Whenever there is contact between yachts it follows that there has been an infringement (although if umpires cannot decide who is to blame they may decide not to penalise either yacht). Perhaps surprisingly, the act of colliding is not in itself an offence, although failing to attempt to avoid a collision resulting in damage may be penalised. In fleet racing, and match racing when sailing your own yachts, the damage has to be 'serious' for there to be an infringement. However, in match racing when the organising authority provide the boats, rule 32 is amended by Appendix B6 such that the yachts are required to attempt to avoid damage. Now, the damage need not be 'serious' for there to be an infringement. This is an important and onerous obligation. Although it is not referred to repetitiously throughout the book, when the rules permit a yacht to 'luff as she pleases', for example, bear in mind that she is at all times obliged to attempt to avoid damage.

Changes to the racing right of way rules

For readers conversant with the racing right of way rules (IYRR Part IV) but not the match racing Appendix B6, here is a list of differences. Firstly there are those that apply to all match races irrespective of whether umpires are used:

■ *Rule 32 (Serious Damage)* As discussed previously, when the yachts are provided by the organising authority, damage, whether serious or minor, is included.

■ *Rule 35 (Limitations on Altering Course)* This rule is rewritten to make it clear that a right of way yacht may alter course provided that she leaves the give way yacht an opportunity to keep clear in a seamanlike manner.

■ *Rule 39.3 (Sailing Below a Proper Course)* This rule does not apply unless there is an overlap and only applies when the windward yacht is within two (rather than three) of her overall lengths of the leeward yacht.

■ New rules are introduced to prevent a yacht deviating from her proper course to interfere with her opponent on another leg of the course or in the act of taking a penalty. The actions of a yacht against yachts in other matches are also limited to those consistent with the yacht winning her own match.

In addition when umpires are used, the following apply:

■ *Fundamental D (Accepting Penalties)* Yachts are not required to take any penalty unless signalled to do so by the umpires.

■ *Definition of finishing* A yacht cannot finish until she has completed any on-the-water penalties imposed by the umpires.

■ *Rule 33 (Contact Between Yachts Racing)* This rule is deleted completely.

■ *Rules 40.1 (Doubt About Mast Abeam), 43 (Room to Tack at Obstructions)* These rules, the only ones that require hails to be made, add hand signals to the requirement.

Two more, one from Part V and one from Part VI are changed:

■ *Rule 52.2 (Exoneration after Touching a Mark)* This rule is deleted so that the penalty becomes the same as any other umpire imposed penalty.

■ *Rule 70.2 (Protest Hearings).* This rule is modified so that hearings cannot be called for infringements of rules that umpires are authorised to decide on the water.

To some extent all the rules of the appendix alter or create differences from the 'standard' yacht racing rules; and as with the rule book itself, there is no substitute for reading the original text.

Interpretation of the racing rules

There can surely be no other sport as complex as yacht racing. Though many sailors believe that the yacht racing rules could be significantly simplified, it would in fact be impossible to do so and still provide a clear indication of yachts' rights and obligations in all but the simplest situations.

The rules come under much scrutiny by those involved in match racing. The International Regulations for Preventing Collisions at Sea (IRPCAS) are framed to keep vessels well apart and reduce as much as is practical the risk of contact; the requirement to anticipate is fundamental. The International Yacht Racing Rules (IYRR), on the other hand, are framed to allow yachts to manoeuvre very closely without contact, and in most situations anticipation of the need to take avoiding action is not required. It follows that the moment at which a yacht becomes obliged to take action (or at which a new obligation is imposed, or an obligation is removed from a yacht) is often critical in any form of yacht racing. In match racing this is especially so because of the increased interaction between the two yachts.

A major problem for the sport of match racing, and to a lesser degree all other forms of yacht racing, is that various judges, umpires and competitors interpret rules differently. There are two main reasons for this. The first is because of a lack of knowledge: it takes time and effort to study the rules and the standard interpretations. The second reason arises from people's differing backgrounds: some are very seamanship oriented and others less so; some like seeing everything in black and white whereas others enjoy balancing rights and obligations.

Many of these problems can be overcome with dialogue and experimentation on the race course, and the growing popularity of match racing has done much to focus on the grey areas and develop common interpretations. Most skippers don't particularly care what interpretations are used, provided they know about them and can depend upon them being the same whatever and wherever they sail.

Early in 1992 the IYRU (International Yacht Racing Union) introduced a book of umpire calls. This is a series of situations that might arise during a match race. For each situation a number of questions are posed, and answers given defining how the umpires should react. The main purpose of the book is to ensure consistency between umpires and is essential material for umpires and skippers alike.

Anticipation

A fundamental difference between the racing rules and the IRPCAS is that, under the racing rules, anticipation, other than mental preparation, is rarely required. Thus, in a situation where the give way and right of way labels are changing, a yacht that becomes newly obliged to give way is normally not under any obligation to take any action to keep clear until she actually becomes the give way yacht; in other words she does not have to anticipate becoming the give way yacht. For example, if Yellow is clear ahead (right of way) with sails flapping and with no way on (ie no movement through the water and therefore no steerage way) and her opponent, Blue, establishes an overlap to leeward, at the instant the overlap is established, Yellow, now a windward yacht, becomes the give way yacht and is required to keep clear. She is required to act promptly, but the fact that she will need time and space to pull in her sheets, slide to leeward until her keel unstalls and swing her transom overhang to leeward as she luffs, will all have to be taken into consideration by Blue; Yellow need take no action until Blue establishes the overlap, even though she knows she will need to do so when the overlap is established.

Skipper's attitude

To win you need to beat your opponent fair and square on-the-water. A fleet race can sometimes be won with a successful 'technical' protest but, using the racing rules Appendix B6 and the procedures developed since 1988, this is very rarely true of a match race. Protesting when you consider your opponent has infringed a 'when yachts meet' racing rule is normal and perfectly acceptable, but protesting about trivia when you have lost a match will cost much time and effort and a protest committee will rarely overturn the on-the-water result. Reversing a fundamental principle in the standard racing rules, the match racing appendix allows the protest committee not to disqualify or penalise a yacht when it finds, at a post-race hearing, that a yacht has infringed a rule, provided it is satisfied that it had no effect on the outcome of the match.

A wise and successful match racing skipper will accept umpires' decisions and, when penalised, focus attention first on taking the penalty efficiently to minimise its detrimental effect and then on overhauling the opponent. Only after the race is finished should the skipper think about the incident and the decision. If unhappy with the decisions, by all means seek out the umpires and discuss it with them. This can do nothing but improve both the skipper's and umpire's understanding of the application of the rules to that situation. (Never can the decision or penalty be changed, though, even were the umpires to accept that they had made an error.)

For the sport of match racing to be popular with the public it needs to have its different characters. As important as the crews are (and many top match racing crew members are champions in their own right), the public needs to be able to get to know the differing characters of the skippers. We need the brash as well as the nice guys. Throwing a tantrum in the cockpit when the spinnaker gets in a tangle, or because the umpires have imposed a penalty thought to be unjustified, is perfectly acceptable. Expressing a view, publicly on shore, that the umpires made an error is also acceptable.

On the other hand, aiming insults or gestures at the umpires is not acceptable as it brings the game into disrepute, and many umpires would not be prepared to serve were they subjected to this kind of abuse. Should such behaviour occur the appendix makes provision for the umpires to be able to impose an immediate penalty. In addition, if the behaviour were extreme or continued for an extended period it would become a 'gross breach of good manners or sportsmanship' to be dealt with under racing rule 75. The penalty for such an infringement may be determined by the protest committee, including disqualification from the regatta. To the credit of the many skippers and crews who have helped develop the sport, there has not yet, to our knowledge, been a rule 75 hearing at a major match race regatta.

Another important skill of a successful match race crew is the ability to lose a race and to bounce back to peak performance a few minutes later. The importance of this becomes apparent when you consider that in each match race there is one winner and one loser. In a fleet race with fifty yachts you may be very pleased to come second by only a few feet, in match racing, you lost! You may win the fleet regatta coming second in every race, but in match racing you come last.

The use of complex tactics dependent upon exploiting controversial rule interpretations should be avoided. This is especially true when umpiring is being used. The umpires can judge only what they see and their decisions will be based invariably on fundamental rules and principles, established case-law and standard tactical scenarios. When umpires are used there is of course no opportunity for a skipper to explain why his yacht was 'in the right' or why the other yacht has infringed.

As with any other form of yacht racing anomalies should be considered as opportunities: shifty winds, obstructions, unusual courses and unusual sailing instructions are all opportunities for the canny skipper, but pitfalls for the unwary.

Unless there is a very good reason for it, a wise skipper will never fail to cover when in the lead, nor miss an opportunity to make life more difficult for his opponent when behind.

Rule 35 (Appendix B6 para 1.2), (Limitations on Altering Course) and the 'avenue of escape'

When two yachts S (on starboard tack) and P (on port tack) are *not* on a collision course, there is no obligation for P to take any action because by doing nothing she is fulfilling her obligation to keep clear. She may, if she wants to, stop still in the water with no steerage way. This is not because she is not obliged to keep clear (rule 36 requires her to keep clear without mentioning whether or not the two yachts are on a collision course), but because to stop dead in the water is one of several options that she may take up in order to fulfil her obligation to keep clear; in other words, stopping dead in the water can be one way of keeping clear.

P may, if she wishes, alter her speed or course (or both) so that the courses of each of the two yachts become a collision course, but P will have to do something (change course or speed, or both) again so that she is no longer on a collision course.

If, on the other hand, S changes course so that the two yachts are on a collision course, she is obliged by rule 35 to do so far enough from P to enable P to keep clear without difficulty. When S alters her course on to a collision course, P becomes obliged to take action to keep clear. If the only avenue of escape is to sail on, then she becomes obliged to sail on. If she has several avenues of escape she may choose any one of them.

If, because of S's change of course, there is no avenue of escape for P (S planning to change course later to avoid contact), then P must take whatever action seems best to make it easy for S to keep clear; this usually means that P should sail on rather than tack.

S may alter course or speed to close all but one avenue of escape, or she may close P's chosen avenue provided that she leaves or opens up another.

Provided she doesn't 'frighten' S into thinking there is going to be contact causing damage, P may leave her 'action' as late as she pleases. The two yachts might be sailing towards each other on a head-on collision course. P has the option of luffing or bearing away. If she waits till the last moment before she changes course and S, fearful of contact, changes course at the same time and there is contact, P will be to blame.

Take again the case of the two yachts sailing towards each other on a head-on collision course. P again has the option of luffing or bearing away, so with plenty of time to spare she chooses to luff. S responds by luffing, closing that avenue of escape but opening (or leaving open) the opportunity for P to bear away to keep clear. P must now take this opportunity as it is the only one left to her.

This principle is fundamental to the game of match racing. The right of way yacht may manoeuvre against the give way yacht and the give way yacht must continue to do whatever is necessary to keep clear.

Whether or not the 'avenue of escape' principle is an interpretation of rule 35, or whether it in fact changes rule 35, has been much debated. The changes to Appendix B6, agreed in November 1991, included a new clause to show that, without doubt, the right of way yacht has the right to manoeuvre against the give way yacht, provided she leaves her room and opportunity to keep clear in a seamanlike manner. Whether or not this actually changes rule 35, the principle has become a universally accepted part of the game.

Rule 42 (Rounding or Passing Marks and Obstructions)

The preamble to section C of the rules, which includes rule 42, and the opening paragraph of rule 42 itself are important because they determine when, and to what extent, rule 42 applies and when it overrides the principal right of way rules (those in section B).

As most racing helmsmen know, rule 42 does not apply between two yachts on opposite tacks on a beat, or when one (but not both) has to tack to round the mark. There are other situations when, although rule 42 applies, it is unnecessary as it is not in conflict with the rules of section B.

WHEN THERE IS NO CONFLICT

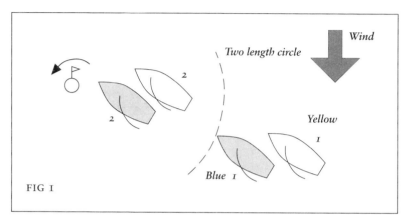

FIG 1

In Fig 1 at position 2, the principal rules require Yellow as windward yacht to keep clear of Blue. If Blue has luffing rights then she may 'luff as she pleases' and Yellow must still keep clear. If Blue does not have luffing rights (she may have come from clear astern some time before the two length circle), then Blue is obliged 'not to sail above her proper course' and, provided that she complies with this obligation, Yellow must still keep clear. Rule 42 requires Yellow to give room to Blue to round the mark, but because this obligation is not in conflict, the principal right of way rules are not overridden and rule 42 becomes effectively redundant. Should there be contact, then umpires or a protest committee would have to be satisfied that Blue didn't have luffing rights and sailed above a proper course before a decision will favour Yellow.

In Fig 2, again the right of way yacht is on the inside, and doesn't need rule 42 because there is no conflict with rules 37 and 39. With luffing rights Blue may sail straight on or luff; without luffing rights Blue must not sail above a proper course and must therefore gybe when her proper course requires a gybe. Again the umpires will need to be satisfied that Blue sailed above, or beyond, her proper course when not entitled to do so before a decision will go against her.

In both these two scenarios, Blue with luffing rights may luff as she pleases and Yellow must keep clear. Whether or not Yellow 'gives

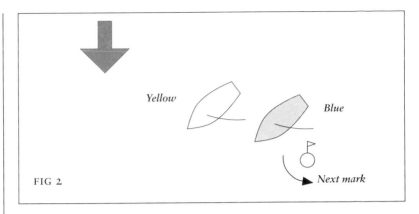

Yellow

Blue

FIG 2

Next mark

room' is irrelevant, and how much room Blue takes is irrelevant. Without luffing rights, Blue must not sail above (or beyond) her proper course. Provided that Blue fulfils that obligation, Yellow must keep clear and Blue need not worry about taking more room than that required to round 'in a seamanlike manner'; she may sail the efficient course she would have sailed in the absence of Yellow.

WHEN THERE IS NO INTENTION TO ROUND ON THE CORRECT SIDE

Fig 3 shows Blue (with luffing rights) and Yellow approaching a mark to be rounded to port. Blue hails to Yellow, "I am intending to pass to windward of the mark; got that? I'm going to the wrong side". The yachts are now not 'about to round the mark on the same required side', a prerequisite for rule 42 to apply. Supporting Blue's case that rule 42 doesn't apply is some case law (IYRU case 37) about a yacht that left a mark on the wrong side, in error, and won her appeal. In addition, the rule that used to require a hail by Blue and the luff before the two length circle was removed in 1989.

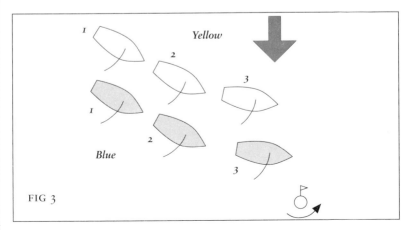

Yellow

Blue

FIG 3

However we strongly recommend that a more satisfactory interpretation of 'about to round' is used: unless Blue has already luffed and is clearly passing the mark on the wrong side when Blue touches the two length circle, she is 'about to round' (whatever her intentions), because she is in a position that would lead any knowledgeable observer to assume that she is about to round the mark.

DO BOTH YACHTS HAVE TO BE 'ABOUT TO ROUND'?

Another problem is with the word 'yachts' (plural) in the opening phrase of rule 42: 'Rule 42 applies when *yachts* are about to round...'. Again the only sensible interpretation for match racing is 'when the leading yacht is "about to round".'

RULE 42 APPLYING WHILE ROUNDING

Lastly, does rule 42 apply while the yachts are in the act of rounding or passing (having passed through the point at which they 'are about to round')? The only interpretation that is workable of the words at the beginning of rule 42 'Rule 42 applies when yachts are about to round or pass...' is: 'Rule 42 begins to apply when yachts are about to round or pass...and continues to apply until the rule is no longer required to override the principal rules to allow the yachts to sail the course or safely negotiate the obstruction.'

2
Terms

It is important that the meaning of certain terms and phrases is understood, especially the definitions in Part I of the racing rules. Some undefined terms and phrases commonly used in match racing are also included here.

The definitions

RACING

Definition: 'A yacht is *racing* from her preparatory signal until she has either *finished* and cleared the finishing line and finishing *marks* or retired, or until the race has been *postponed, abandoned,* or a general recall has been signalled.'

Yachts are subject to Part IV of the racing rules (Right of Way Rules - Rights and Obligations when Yachts Meet) before and after the race, but can be penalised for infringing a rule of Part IV only if the infringement occurs while racing. The rules of Part V (Other Sailing Rules - Obligations in Handling a Yacht) are applicable only while racing.

Clearing the finishing line simply means getting all of the yacht and its equipment clear of the line. In practice it is more usual to get everything on to the post-course side of the line, but either side will do. Clearing the finishing marks is more difficult to interpret, but generally it is taken to mean that the yacht is in no danger of fouling a finishing mark.

Having cleared the line and cleared the marks, should a yacht come back and hit a finishing mark she would not be penalised, since it is not possible to 'recommence' racing.

If a yacht finishes, clears the line, and then immediately hits a finishing mark, she would not have ceased racing and would need to take the penalty for hitting the mark, and then finish. Of course only her second crossing of the finishing line counts.

If a yacht finishes some distance from both finishing marks, clears the line by getting the whole boat over, or behind, the line, then she has, at that moment, also cleared the finishing marks. If after that moment she infringes a racing rule she would not be penalised.

STARTING

Definition: 'A yacht starts when, after fulfilling her penalty obligations, if any, under 51.1(c), and after her starting signal, any part of her hull, crew or equipment first crosses the starting line in the direction of the course to the first mark.'

Thus a yacht cannot start before her starting signal, and what is known (and described in the racing rules) as a 'premature starter' is a yacht that has crossed the starting line in the right direction but before the starting signal. Such a yacht is accorded the rights of a yacht that has started correctly until it is obvious that she is returning to start. Then she must keep clear of all yachts that have started correctly, until she has wholly returned to the pre-start side of the starting line, or its extensions, when she regains her rights.

When, as is not uncommon in match racing, both yachts are 'premature starters' and both are returning to start, until one yacht is wholly on the pre-start side of the starting line, the rules are applied between them as if they were not returning. This can lead to some rapid changes of right of way and requires umpires to be very alert. But remember that when one yacht acquires rights she must allow the newly obligated yacht room and opportunity to keep clear.

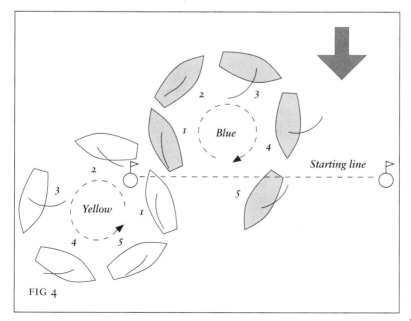

FIG 4

In Fig 4, Blue and Yellow are both premature starters. At position 1, Blue (windward) is required to keep clear of Yellow (leeward). At position 2 it is clear that Yellow is returning to start and must now keep clear as must Blue at position 3, should either be at risk of fouling their opponent. Soon after position 3 Yellow has wholly returned to the pre-start extension of the starting line and thus regains her rights. At position 5, Blue has yet to clear the starting line and cannot use her starboard rights, thus she must keep clear of Yellow. Even when she clears the line, Blue must give Yellow room and opportunity to keep clear.

FINISHING

Definition: When umpires are used this definition is amended to read 'A yacht *finishes* when any part of her hull, or of her crew or equipment in normal position, crosses the finishing line in the direction of the course from the last *mark*, after fulfilling any penalty obligations signalled for infringements occurring when racing.

Suppose that there is an incident close to the finishing line such that the yachts cross the line before the umpires have time to signal a penalty. What happens? The answer is that it is the time of the infringement that is important, not the time of umpire signal imposing the penalty. In this case the yacht is required to complete the penalty, return wholly to the course side and then cross the finishing line in accordance with the definition.

Similarly, a yacht might finish but then touch a finishing mark, whereupon she retrospectively fails to fulfil the definition of finishing. This is one case when a yacht may be well advised not to wait for the umpires to signal a penalty as the sooner she completes the penalty the sooner she will finish and hence the greater her chance of winning the match (Fig 5).

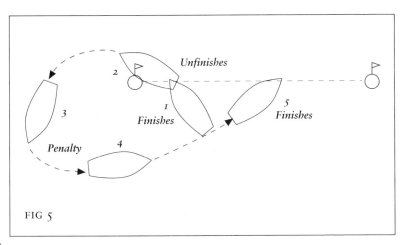

FIG 5

LUFFING

Definition: 'Altering course towards the wind.'

That's simple enough; a yacht cannot luff *beyond* head-to-wind, because at the moment she passes *through* head-to-wind she is tacking. Sometimes, when luffing up to head-to-wind and hovering, whether or not a yacht has passed through head-to-wind can be vitally important. While she hovers, provided she has not passed through the eye of the wind, she remains on the tack she was on before she luffed. If she inadvertently passes through head-to-wind (even if caused by a wind shift) and then goes back to head-to-wind, she is tacking. She will continue to be tacking until she bears away, one way or the other, on to a close hauled course.

TACKING

Definition: 'A yacht is *tacking* from the moment she is beyond head-to-wind until she has *borne away* to a *close hauled course*.'

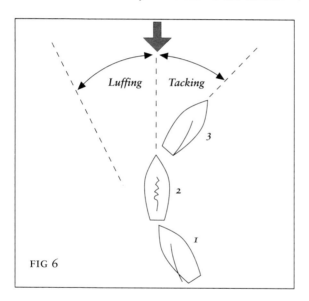

FIG 6

'A close hauled course' is generally accepted as being the course a yacht would be steering were she at full speed, on-the-wind in the prevailing conditions, rather than the direction to which she chooses to bear away to gain speed after a tack. Fig 6 shows a yacht luffing up to head-to-wind and then tacking.

Fig 7 shows a yacht luffing through head-to-wind, then turning back to her original tack.

Fig 8 shows the same manoeuvre except that the yacht does not pass through head-to-wind and therefore never ceases to be on starboard tack.

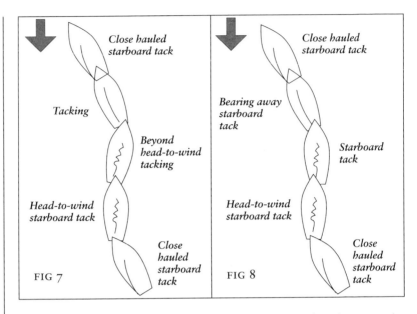

Tacking		Close hauled starboard tack
	Beyond head-to-wind tacking	
Head-to-wind starboard tack		
FIG 7		Close hauled starboard tack

	Close hauled starboard tack
Bearing away starboard tack	Starboard tack
Head-to-wind starboard tack	
FIG 8	Close hauled starboard tack

In all these cases it is only the position of the yacht relative to the wind direction that has any meaning within the rules. What is happening to the sails (full or not) or the boom is irrelevant.

At the moment a yacht passes through head-to-wind she is tacking; if, instead of completing her tack, she luffs again to head-to-wind, then she remains in the state of 'tacking' until she has borne away, one way or the other, to a close hauled course. Thus, two yachts may be hovering head-to-wind, and only if it is known how they got there could it be known that one was 'tacking' while the other was 'on a tack' (port or starboard), or both tacking, or they were on opposite tacks, or both on the same tack!

It is not easy for crew or umpires to judge when a yacht has just gone through head-to-wind. If in doubt umpires should determine that a yacht has not begun tacking, and therefore is still 'on a tack'. It is unsafe to base a judgement on whether the genoa clew (or any other part of the sails for that matter) has crossed the centreline because of: the tendency for sails to whip both sides of centre when head-to-wind; the apparent wind effect as the yacht is turning; and the momentum of the sails as the yacht stops turning. A masthead indicator suffers from the apparent wind effects because of the motion of the yacht laterally and the mast swinging whereas it is the relationship of the hull to the true wind direction that is the determining factor.

BEARING AWAY

Definition: 'Altering course away from the wind until a yacht begins to gybe.'

Strictly speaking, if a yacht bears away until she is sailing dead downwind, and then continues turning in the same direction say another 5 degrees so that she is sailing by the lee, the last 5 degrees of her turn were luffing because she is turning towards the wind. In fact in most wind strengths any yacht other than a dinghy or a sailboard will need to pass through dead downwind and 'luff' a little before it can initiate a gybe. However, it would be unwise to try to invent tactics that depended upon this phenomenon, as all sensible judges will interpret the rule such that a yacht is continuing to bear away until the foot of the mainsail crosses the centreline of the yacht.

GYBING

Definition: 'A yacht begins to *gybe* at the moment when, with the wind aft, the foot of her mainsail crosses her centreline, and completes the *gybe* when the mainsail has filled on the other tack.'

Unlike tacking, a gybe is normally completed within an insignificant amount of time, an important fact in many match racing tactical manoeuvres.

ON A TACK

Definition: 'A yacht is *on a tack* except when she is *tacking* or *gybing*. A yacht is *on the tack (starboard)* or *(port)* corresponding to her *windward* side.'

By looking also at the definition of 'windward side', we see that this has little to do with which side of the yacht the wind is striking, but the side on which the mainsail is being carried.

Whenever a yacht is running by the lee her windward side, by definition, is not the same side as that which the wind is striking. The reason why the rule is written this way is that while it is relatively easy to see on which side she is carrying her mainsail and hence which yacht holds the right of way, it is almost impossible to determine exactly when the yacht starts, or ceases, to run by the lee.

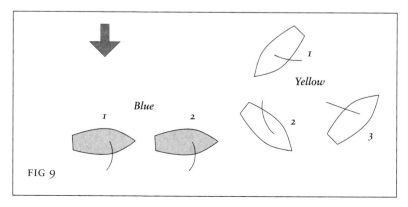

FIG 9

ON A TACK, WITH THE MAINSAIL BACKED

Suppose that it was Yellow running by the lee and that she continues to 'bear away' but restrains her boom from moving as in Fig 9.

She hasn't gybed because she hasn't fulfilled the definition of gybing that requires the boom to cross the centreline. However, at position 2 her mainsail is fully backed and but for her boom being restrained she would be carrying her mainsail on her starboard side. She is therefore on port tack and as windward yacht is required to keep clear.

Now look at Fig 10. In position 1, Yellow is close hauled on port tack. There is only a light wind blowing and, in order to stop, she hauls the boom across the centreline to achieve a similar position to Yellow (3) in Fig 9. She remains on port tack for the same reason, her mainsail is only on her port side because of the actions of the crew, not the action of the wind.

Thus, especially in light winds, a yacht may change tack (from port to starboard, for example), without gybing, simply by restraining the boom from crossing the centreline and altering course sufficiently for the mainsail to become fully backed. It is quite common when sailing upwind, again in light airs, to set the boom above the centreline, but again it is only the restraint on the boom that prevents all the mainsail from being carried on the port side. In Fig 11 the yacht is on starboard tack.

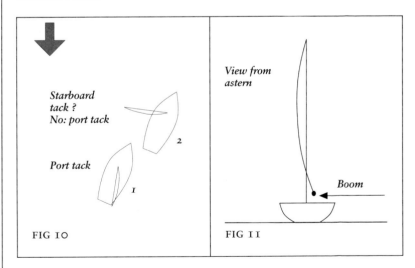

Starboard
tack ?
No: port tack

Port tack

1

2

FIG 10

View from
astern

Boom

FIG 11

When a yacht pushes her boom out to leeward and backs the mainsail in order to stop she remains on the same tack because even when the boom were let go the mainsail remains carried on the same side.

It may be that a more satisfactory definition of *leeward/windward* would read as follows;

'The *leeward* side of a yacht is the side that her unrestrained mainsail is carried, or if restrained would be carried when unrestrained, or when the yacht is head-to-wind was being carried. The other side is her *windward* side.'

CLOSE HAULED

Definition: 'A yacht is *close hauled* when sailing by the wind as close as she can lie with advantage in working to windward.'

The angle from the wind will obviously vary with the type of yacht, the wind and wave conditions, but is usually accepted as being the angle from the wind that a yacht would sail in the current conditions were she sailing at best speed made good, rather than the lower (further from the wind) course she might choose to adopt because of her current low speed or immediately after completing a tack.

LEEWARD AND WINDWARD

Definition: 'The *leeward* side of a yacht is that on which she is, or when head to wind, was, carrying her mainsail. The opposite side is the *windward* side. When neither of two yachts on the same tack is *clear astern*, the one on the *leeward* side of the other is the *leeward* yacht. The other is the *windward* yacht.'

As we have seen when looking at 'on a tack', 'carrying her mainsail' is not synonymous with 'carrying her boom'. A yacht hoping to change tack simply by hauling the boom over the centreline will not be able to get the mainsail to be carried on its unnatural side.

PROPER COURSE

Definition: 'A *proper course* is any course that a yacht might *sail* after the starting signal, in the absence of the other yacht or yachts affected to *finish* as quickly as possible. There is no *proper course* before the starting signal.'

This definition is important and deserves close scrutiny. The wording of the definition is clear: a yacht, permitted by the rules to sail her proper course, can ignore the other yacht provided she doesn't make any sudden, unexpected changes of course. Unfortunately the decision in IYRU case 97 goes against this principle, which makes the rule more difficult to interpret and apply. In case 97, a leeward yacht (say Blue) without luffing rights and sailing a parallel course to a windward yacht (say Yellow) had a spinnaker problem; without the spinnaker Blue's best course was higher than it was with the spinnaker, and higher than Yellow's best course. Blue changed course gradually to the higher course and sailed some five boat lengths, converging while Yellow held a steady course. There was contact. The ruling was that Blue should have held her original course as she was not entitled to use a temporary condition to justify a luff, particularly when that condition was caused by her own poor seamanship or sail handling. No doubt if Blue had simply taken down her spinnaker for the remainder of the leg the decision would have gone in her favour. You may have detected that we don't agree with the ruling.

There is no doubt, though, that a leeward yacht without luffing rights may luff and bear away on waves, and sail the course *she* believes would be the best for her, in the absence of W.

It is important to bear in mind that 'proper course' is only relevant when the two yachts are on the same tack after the starting signal. Even then, a yacht is never required to sail or not sail to her proper course; only that in certain circumstances a yacht is required not to sail *below* or not to sail *above* her proper course, or is required to *return* to a course *not above*, or *not below*, a proper course.

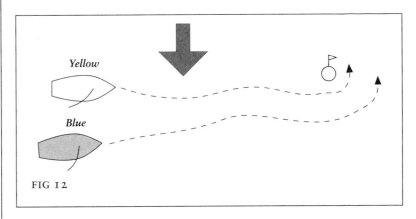

FIG 12

There are several situations in which umpires have to judge whether a yacht is sailing above or below her proper course. They will generally give the benefit of the doubt to the yacht whose proper course is in question.

In Fig 12 both proper courses are relevant. Blue, without luffing rights may sail up to her proper course, until she or Yellow are 'about to round' the mark (position x), at which time Blue must give room to Yellow. Provided Blue gives room for Yellow to round in a seamanlike manner, Yellow continues to be obliged to keep clear. Yellow must not sail below her proper course at any time.

In diagram 13, Blue and Yellow are heading for the mark and the obligation on Yellow to keep clear (as windward yacht) is dominant. In the absence of a tidal stream, Yellow's proper course (ignoring variations to ride waves) can never be below the mark, even if the wind speed changed, but Blue's proper course could change to being above the mark if the wind speed decreased. This is because the

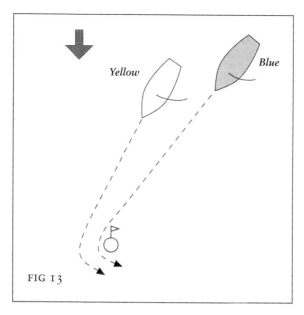

FIG 13

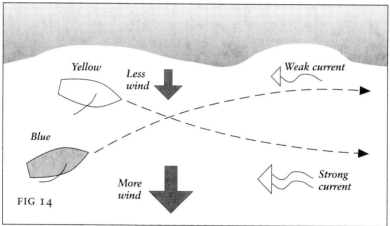

FIG 14

higher course would give her best VMG (velocity made good), her most efficient downwind course.

If there is a protest, unless the umpires are positively satisfied that Blue has sailed above a proper course, or that Yellow has sailed below a proper course, they will not penalise either yacht on those issues, leaving the issue only of whether Yellow, as windward yacht kept clear.

In Fig 14, the yachts' opinions as to what is the proper course vary greatly, but again both proper courses are relevant in that Yellow must not sail below her proper course and Blue (without luffing rights) must not sail above hers. Yellow must keep clear (Blue will have to give room if Yellow is overlapped inside when they get to the shore).

With umpires, the yachts do not get the opportunity they have in a protest room to 'justify' their proper course. The umpires should be constantly addressing the issue and looking for reasons that would justify the course the yachts are sailing: current, gusts, wind bends, shifts, increases or decreases, obstructions. In this way they will be ready to give a decision in the event of a protest. However vigilant the umpires may be in looking for these justifications, it is inevitable that some of the more bizarre factors will be overlooked. This has the effect of limiting some of the extreme 'proper courses'; wise skippers will take this into account while racing.

When Blue has luffing rights her proper course is irrelevant.

MARK

Definition: 'A *mark* is any object specified in the sailing instructions that a yacht must round or pass on a required side. Ground tackle and any object either accidentally or temporarily attached to the *mark* are not part of it.

A mark can also be an obstruction, for example a committee boat used as one end of the starting or finishing line.

OBSTRUCTION

Definition: 'An *obstruction* is any object, including a vessel under way, large enough to require a yacht, when more than one overall length away from it, to make a substantial alteration of course to pass on one side or the other, or any object that can be passed on one side only, including a buoy when the yacht in question cannot safely pass between it and the shoal or the object that it marks. The sailing instructions may prescribe that a specified area shall rank as an *obstruction*.'

A mid course starting/finishing line that is specified in the sailing instructions as having to be passed on either side (in other words yachts may not pass through it) is an obstruction. It could be argued that the starting/finishing line is not an 'object', so it is best for the race committee wishing to specify that yachts do not go through the line to include in the sailing instructions the words 'the area between the buoy displaying the red flag and the committee boat ranks as an obstruction'.

CLEAR ASTERN AND CLEAR AHEAD; OVERLAP

Definition: 'A yacht is *clear astern* of another when her hull and equipment in normal position are abaft an imaginary line projected abeam from the aftermost point of the other's hull and equipment in normal position. The other yacht is *clear ahead*.

The yachts *overlap* when neither is *clear astern*; or when, although one is *clear astern*, an intervening yacht *overlaps* both of them.

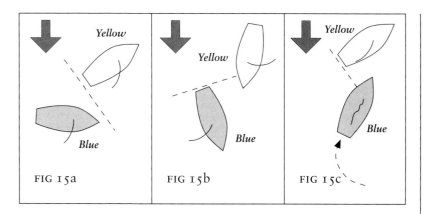

FIG 15a   FIG 15b   FIG 15c

The terms *clear astern*, *clear ahead* and *overlap* apply to yachts on opposite *tacks* only when they are subject to rule 42.

The critical line at right angles to the fore-aft line is taken from 'the aftermost point' which might be the rudder under water in the case of a dinghy or small keel boat, or an aerial etc.

In Fig 15a, yacht Blue is clear astern, therefore Yellow must be clear ahead.

In Fig 15b, the yachts are overlapped, but because they are on opposite tacks, the fact that they are overlapped is irrelevant unless they are about to round or pass a mark or obstruction.

In Fig 15c, Blue is tacking and therefore not 'on the same tack' and again the overlap is irrelevant. Nor are they on opposite tacks so the overlap is irrelevant even when subject to rule 42.

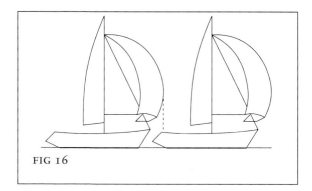

FIG 16

In determining whether a yacht has an overlap, the position of the spinnaker, often billowing ahead of the stem will be the determining factor, provided it is flying in its normal position (Fig 16).

When deciding whether or not an overlap exists, there will be times when there is doubt. The umpires will determine what the situation was before there was any doubt. If there was no overlap, they will assume there is no overlap until they are satisfied that one exists; if there was an overlap they will assume that the overlap continues until they are satisfied that it has been broken. In this way the clauses of rule 42 containing the onuses of satisfying the protest committee are handled in a very similar manner when umpires are used.

MAST ABEAM

Definition: 'A *windward* yacht *sailing* no higher than a *leeward* yacht is *mast abeam* when her helmsman's line of sight abeam from his normal station is forward of the *leeward* yacht's mainmast. A *windward* yacht *sailing* higher than a *leeward* yacht is *mast abeam* when her helmsman's line of sight abeam from his normal *station* would be, if she were *sailing* no higher, forward of the *leeward* yacht's mainmast.'

To understand the principles of gaining and losing luffing rights it is essential to know what is meant by the 'mast abeam' position. The term applies only to the windward yacht of two overlapping yachts on the same tack.

What is a 'normal station' is rarely a problem. A helmsman would not be in normal position if immediately before making his claim he moved significantly forward in the boat. It would be his normal position, however, if that forward position was the one he normally adopted on a similar leg of the course in similar conditions.

Fig 17a shows two yachts sailing parallel courses, with Yellow in a mast abeam position. In Fig 17b, Yellow's course is lower than Blue's

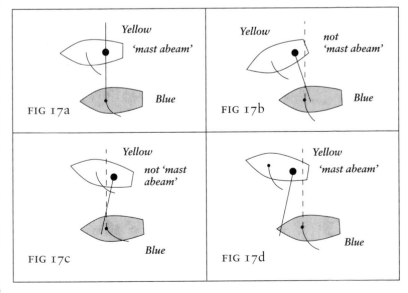

FIG 17a — Yellow 'mast abeam' / Blue

FIG 17b — Yellow not 'mast abeam' / Blue

FIG 17c — Yellow not 'mast abeam' / Blue

FIG 17d — Yellow 'mast abeam' / Blue

course. The line abeam from Yellow's helmsman is abaft the mast of Blue, so Yellow is not 'mast abeam', but if she luffed a little she would be.

In Fig 17c, Yellow's course is higher than Blue's course, but if she were sailing no higher than Blue then her helmsman's line of sight abeam would be behind Blue's mainmast. Yellow is not mast abeam.

In Fig 17d, Yellow's course is again higher than Blue's course. However, even if Yellow's course were no higher than Blue's her helmsman's line of sight abeam would be in front of the mast of Blue. Yellow is mast abeam.

In a luffing match in which Blue luffs Yellow quickly and Yellow is eager to attain mast abeam to negate further luffing, Yellow's helmsman will sight abeam and, seeing Blue's mast will often think his yacht has attained the mast-abeam position when in fact it hasn't.

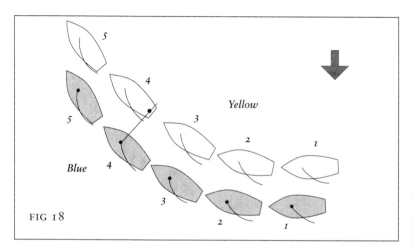

FIG 18

Fig 18, position 1, shows Yellow gaining an overlap to windward of Blue. At postion 2, Blue luffs and Yellow responds. By position 4, Yellow is mast abeam and may hail 'Mast abeam' and give the hand signal; Blue must immediately bear away to her proper course, or below.

If Yellow does not hail mast abeam at position 4, Blue is permitted 'to assume she has the right to luff' if 'there is doubt'. 'If there is doubt' means if Blue's helmsman, acting reasonably, is not sure that Yellow has achieved the mast-abeam position. Consequently, if Yellow has not hailed mast abeam, and Blue continues to luff as in position 5, a protest by Yellow will not succeed. It follows that it is tactically advantageous for Yellow to monitor carefully the relative positions and hail mast abeam at the very moment she is mast abeam. Yellow must also be aware that an early hail may cause Blue to protest and the umpires to penalise her.

Rule 40.1 requires that the helmsman makes the hail. Should a member of the crew other than the helmsman make the hail, the leeward yacht can ignore it and keep luffing (if the helmsman is reasonably in doubt).

In an interesting case in Fremantle during the Americas Cup defence trials in December 1986, *Australia* and *Kookaburra* were reaching overlapped with *Australia* to windward. In spite of being mast abeam, *Australia's* helmsman did not hail, and as it was close *Australia* did not achieve a position where the helmsman of *Kookaburra* (Iain Murray) was in no doubt that he had lost luffing rights. *Kookaburra* then gained on *Australia* and Iain, thinking he had luffing rights, luffed hard. *Australia's* helmsman now hailed "Mast abeam" even though *Australia* was now abaft the mast abeam position. *Kookaburra* bore away and protested for an improper hail. The protest committee decided that because *Australia* had been mast abeam some time earlier, while the same overlap existed, the hail was legitimate and dismissed the protest.

That was before the days of umpiring; it is doubtful that umpires would make the same decision. Unless there has been a hail at a time when the windward helmsman is mast-abeam, or it is obvious that the windward yacht has achieved mast-abeam, umpires are most likely to be of the opinion that the leeward yacht has luffing rights, and a hail of 'Mast abeam' when not mast abeam will result in a penalty for the windward yacht should the leeward yacht protest.

A wise helmsman of the windward yacht will always hail and signal when mast abeam, even if the leeward yacht is not luffing or is unlikely to luff. This precaution should be taken every time there is a new overlap, when tacking upwind for instance.

ROOM

Definition: 'Room is the space needed by a yacht to manoeuvre in a seamanlike manner in the prevailing conditions'.

'Room' is normally less than the space a yacht would like to take, for example, to make a perfect mark rounding. However, a yacht is entitled to sufficient space to ensure that she is able to keep clear of a mark or a yacht giving room. As we will discuss later, 'keeping clear' will normally be more than simply avoiding contact and an inside yacht is permitted to take into consideration that a mark is, for example, heavy and made of metal or that the conditions are rough. Although she is not permitted by this rule to take room for tactical advantage, when it is in question as to whether the inside yacht took too much room, umpires and protest committees will be inclined to give the inside yacht the benefit of any doubt.

The rules never require a yacht to manoeuvre or to be handled in a seamanlike manner. If a give way yacht fails to keep clear of a right of way yacht that has given sufficient room then the give way yacht infringes the basic rule.

Undefined terms

There are some additional terms and phrases not defined in Part I of the racing rules, but which are often used.

CLEAR AIR

This is what every yacht strives to be in! It is wind which is free of disturbance from an opponent's sails, or other objects.

DIRTY AIR, BAD AIR, DIRTY WIND, BACKWIND, WIND SHADOW

Wind disturbed and made turbulent by passing over sails, or any other object, adversely affecting a yacht is 'dirty' or 'bad'. The area of disturbed air to leeward of a yacht's sails is a wind shadow; the yacht so affected is said to be 'in dirty wind', 'in the wind shadow of', 'in bad air', 'gasping' or 'gassed' etc. Wind bent by sails causing an opponent close to a yacht's windward side to be headed, is 'backwind'.

RIGHT OF WAY; GIVE WAY

Although Part IV of the rules is headed 'Right of Way Rules', none of the rules in Part IV (or any other part of the rules for that matter) actually confers right of way on a yacht. One is left to deduce that if Yellow is required to keep clear of Blue, then Blue holds right of way over Yellow, or Blue is the right of way yacht, and Yellow must be the give way yacht. Thus it is safe to assume, although in any given situation each yacht may have certain other rights and will certainly have some obligations, that the yacht holding right of way is determined by the relevant rule in section B (Principle Right of Way Rules and their Limitations). Thus an outside leeward yacht at a mark is the right of way yacht even though she may be required to give room, and the inside yacht remains the give way yacht even though she has the right to room.

When a yacht holds right of way it means that, with certain important exceptions and limitations, she may hold her course, or change her course, causing the other yacht to alter course to keep clear. The other yacht is the give way yacht and is required to 'keep clear' (another undefined term which will be covered in a moment). A give way yacht is not always required to take action to keep clear; for example, when Blue and Yellow overlapped on the same tack are converging, with Blue to leeward sailing above her proper course without luffing rights, Yellow may hold her course. If contact occurs, only Blue will be at fault, even though she is the right of way yacht. This is not because she caused the contact per se, but because she sailed above her proper course. Yellow would still be wise to take action to keep clear and protest.

COLLISION COURSE

Yachts are on a collision course when, if both yachts continue on their current courses and speeds, contact will result. Until the two yachts are within a few boat lengths of each other, it is usually difficult to tell from a position other than on board one of the yachts whether or not they are on a collision course. Umpires frequently have to make such a judgement because usually only when the two yachts are on a collision course does the give way yacht become obliged to take evasive action.

MANOEUVRING AGAINST AN OPPONENT;
ACTING TO INTERFERE WITH

A yacht manoeuvres against another yacht when she alters course with the intention of causing the other yacht to have to alter course, either to avoid infringing a rule or to obtain clear air. This would also be 'acting to interfere with' the other yacht. A yacht would also be 'acting to interfere with' another yacht if she held her course beyond her own proper course to affect the other yacht, but this would not be a 'manoeuvre'.

The match racing appendix (para 1.4) prohibits a yacht from 'deliberately acting to interfere with' a yacht on another leg of the course, or a penalised yacht that is getting clear and while she is exonerating herself, unless sailing a proper course.

This means, for example, that Yellow, sailing close hauled on a starboard tack, causing Blue, running on port to alter course to avoid contact does not infringe, provided that she is at all times sailing her proper course. She may even tack on to starboard quite close to Blue, provided that she does not infringe rule 41 (tacking too close).

When a yacht meets a yacht in another match, Appendix B6 para 1.5 requires that they may only alter course either to fulfil their obligations to keep clear or consistent with winning their own match. For instance, a series of close covering tacks, at significantly greater frequency than in the absence of the other yacht, would infringe the rule, but manoeuvring to establish an inside overlap would not infringe.

Unlike para 1.4, para 1.5 is not open to decisions on-the-water. It requires a post race hearing so a skipper thus accused has the opportunity to explain his actions. This also avoids the problem of umpires allocated to different matches being required to make 'joint' decisions.

KEEP CLEAR

The obligation of a give way yacht, in most situations, is to 'keep clear'. Defining the term 'keep clear' is not easy, and is certainly not always synonymous with 'avoiding contact'. A port tack yacht crossing the bow of a starboard tack, close hauled yacht in high winds and heavy sea, and missing her by a few inches is obviously avoiding contact but certainly not 'keeping clear'. However, when match racing in wind and waves that allow the yachts to miss each other in safety by an inch it is accepted that 'keeping clear' means taking an option that will avoid contact without the other yacht having to alter course to contribute to the avoiding of contact.

In most situations, rule 35 requires that the right of way yacht does not limit the actions of a yacht required to 'keep clear', unless she gives room and opportunity to do so in a seamanlike manner.

When there is more than one option open to the give way yacht she may select any of them; if the right of way yacht alters course to close the chosen option, then she must leave open another option, or create a new one. The give way yacht must then take the option left open to her. If the sole option being taken is closed, the give way yacht should continue as if it were open because rule 35 will have the effect of requiring the right of way yacht to take action to keep clear.

TWO LENGTH CIRCLE

This is an imaginary, critical line around a mark or obstruction, two boat lengths from it. Although the term 'two length circle' is an oft-used phrase, the word circle is really a misnomer since the distance of two lengths is of importance only when approaching a mark or obstruction; it is irrelevant when the yachts have rounded or passed it.

ABOUT TO ROUND

'About to round' is a very important position near a mark or obstruction when rule 42 starts to apply. It is generally accepted as being the point at which a yacht needs to begin preparations for rounding, for example, dowse the spinnaker. Only in the case of yachts making little way over the ground against an adverse tide or current would this position be less than two lengths, but with or without a beneficial stream the distance could be several, or even many, boat lengths.

As yachts approach a mark, umpires should agree when the 'about to round' position has been reached (perhaps by the exchange of words '42 now?' and 'Agreed'). It would certainly be simplest if, for match racing, two boat lengths were to be the standard distance at which the leading boat is considered to be 'about to round', but in heavy weather, for example, this will sometimes be unworkable.

OVERALL LENGTHS

Rule 42 contains several references to boat lengths (or, more exactly, 'two of her overall lengths'). An 'overall length' is the distance between the aftermost part of the hull or permanent structure (such as a pushpit), not including radio aerials and the like, and the forwardmost part of the hull or permanent structure (such as a pulpit, or permanent bowsprit), not including a spinnaker, or a movable bowsprit or pole. An 'overlap' is a different matter, in which spinnakers and the like can indeed be relevant (see the definition of 'overlap' on page 28).

CONTINUING OBSTRUCTION

Rule 42.3(b) gives examples of a continuing obstruction as 'a shoal or the shore or another vessel'. The effect of the difference between a continuing obstruction and an obstruction that is not a continuing one (such as a committee boat or large mark) is that in the latter case, the yacht claiming the right to inside room has to establish her overlap outside two lengths. In the case of the continuing obstruction, when one yacht is more likely to catch the other over a period of time, the overlap must be established at a time when there is room for her to pass 'in safety' between the outer yacht and the obstruction.

In practice, there is rarely a problem with having to decide whether or not an obstruction is a continuing one.

PASS IN SAFETY; SAFE PILOTAGE

Rule 42.3(b), Limitation When an Obstruction is a Continuing One says: 'When yachts are passing a continuous *obstruction*, such as a shoal, or the shore or another vessel, rule 42.3(a)(ii) does not apply, and a yacht *clear astern* may establish an *overlap* between a yacht *clear ahead* and the *obstruction*, provided, at that time, there is *room* for her to *pass in safety*.

This is an unusual rule because a yacht simply establishing an overlap when there is not room to pass in safety thus infringes the rule, and if there is a protest a penalty will be imposed. Who is to decide whether or not there is room to pass in safety? It must surely be the yacht in danger, that is, the inside yacht. However, this leads to some complications; the relevant scenarios are discussed in Chapter 8 about downwind legs.

The words 'safe pilotage' appear in rule: Rule 43.1, Hailing: 'When two *close-hauled* yachts are on the same *tack* and *safe pilotage* requires the yacht *clear ahead* or the *leeward* yacht to make a substantial alteration of course to clear an *obstruction*, and when she intends to *tack*, but cannot *tack* without colliding with the other yacht, she shall hail the other yacht for room to *tack* and clear the other yacht, but she shall not hail and *tack* simultaneously.'

Again, although the yacht hailing for room to tack must have a justifiable reason for believing that she is running into danger, it is up to her to decide the point at which 'safe pilotage' requires her to take action. She is entitled to take into account the reaction time required for the response by any affected yacht.

In all cases, when there is doubt in the minds of the umpires (or the protest committee), the benefit should go to the inside yacht, the yacht establishing the overlap at a continuing obstruction, or the yacht hailing for room to tack.

LAYLINE

When sailing to windward, a course that just fetches a mark, or other object, without tacking is called a 'layline'(Fig 19a). When running in all but the strongest winds, most yachts achieve their best downwind performance by sailing higher than dead downwind to keep the sails unstalled; in very light winds this angle from dead downwind can be dramatic; IACC yachts in 5 knots true wind achieve their best VMG course between 40 and 50 degrees from dead downwind giving a gybe angle of 100 degrees. A downwind VMG course which leads to a mark is also referred to as a 'layline' (Fig 19b).

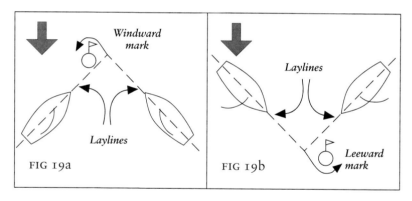

FIG 19a

Windward mark

Laylines

FIG 19b

Laylines

Leeward mark

THE SAFE (STARTING) TRIANGLE

This is the imaginary triangle formed by the starting line, the port tack starboard end layline, and the starboard tack, port end layline (Fig 20).

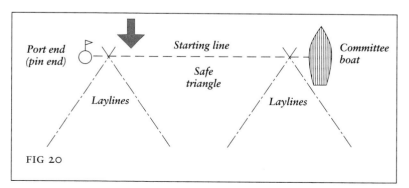

Port end (pin end)

Starting line

Committee boat

Safe triangle

Laylines

Laylines

FIG 20

SLAM DUNK

The manoeuvre of a yacht (Yellow in Fig 21) on a windward leg, crossing ahead of her opponent and tacking close to windward on her wind, compelling her to take action to clear her wind lest she suffer in the tacking yacht's wind shadow, is known as a slam dunk.

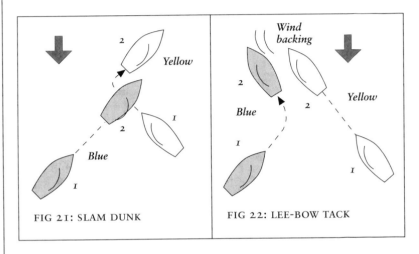

FIG 21: SLAM DUNK   FIG 22: LEE-BOW TACK

TO LEE-BOW

To lee-bow is to tack close under the leeward bow of an opponent (as Blue in Fig 22), so that Yellow is backwinded and is therefore encouraged to tack.

TO LUFF A YACHT

To alter course towards the wind, forcing a yacht to windward to alter course to fulfil her obligation to keep clear.

LUFFING RIGHTS

This is a frequently used, and important, term applied to a leeward yacht or a yacht clear ahead. It means the right to luff above a proper course (or before starting and clearing the starting line, above close hauled) to head-to-wind, causing another yacht to have to alter course to keep clear. The term 'luffing rights' is relevant only when the two yachts are on the same tack.

The acquiring and losing of luffing rights is quite different before the start and after the luffing yacht has started and cleared the starting line.

When match racing, whether a yacht does or does not have luffing rights is a matter of vital importance to the helmsmen of both yachts and to the umpires controlling the match.

1. Luffing rights - before the leeward yacht starts and clears the starting line:

In the pre-start a yacht clear ahead always has luffing rights. A leeward yacht has luffing rights when the windward yacht is abaft mast abeam, and loses luffing rights when the windward yacht is at or forward of mast abeam.

Thus, in the pre-start, luffing rights can come and go during the existence of an overlap as the windward yacht falls behind, then regains mast-abeam.

When the helmsman of the leeward yacht is in doubt he may assume he has luffing rights unless the helmsman of the windward yacht hails and signals 'mast abeam'. Thereafter the leeward yacht regains luffing rights when her helmsman is in no doubt that the windward yacht is no longer mast abeam.

Before starting and clearing the starting line, should the leeward yacht exercise her right to luff, and the other yacht has to alter course to avoid a collision, the luff must be 'carried out slowly and initially in such a way as to give the windward yacht room and opportunity to keep clear'.

The leeward yacht may luff up to close hauled at any time, even if she establishes her overlap from clear astern. If the windward yacht is ahead of mast abeam and would have to alter course to keep clear the leeward yacht may not sail above close hauled. If the leeward yacht is sailing above close hauled when she becomes close enough for the windward yacht to have to respond to keep clear she infringes rule 38.1. The leeward yacht must bear away to a close hauled course, or lower, before then.

This is a change from the previous rule book and will cause significant changes to pre-start manoeuvres.

2. Luffing rights - after starting and clearing the starting line

Again, a yacht clear ahead always has luffing rights. When overlapped, the issue is not so simple. The rules say that there are a number of ways in which a new overlap starts. They are:

- when a yacht that was astern becomes overlapped

- when either of the yachts completes a tack or a gybe

- when the yachts come to within two lengths of each other

- when the leading yacht starts

Also, an overlap, for the purposes of luffing rights, exists only for yachts that are on the same tack.

Similar to starting new overlaps, a particular overlap ends when either yacht becomes clear ahead, when either tacks or gybes, or when the yachts are separated by two lengths or more.

Each overlap is considered separately and the leeward yacht has luffing rights provided that at no time during that particular overlap the windward yacht has achieved mast abeam.

For example, if Yellow is astern and then overtakes on the windward side, Blue will have luffing rights until Yellow achieves mast abeam.

Another example is when Yellow is sailing close hauled on port tack. Blue, on starboard, crosses her bow and then tacks to windward of Yellow's bow. At the instant Blue completes her tack she is ahead of mast abeam but is sailing slowly out of the tack. Even when Yellow ceases to be mast abeam Blue does not have luffing rights and will never have luffing rights until she is either clear ahead or a new overlap starts when Yellow is not mast abeam.

After starting and clearing the starting line, a leeward yacht with luffing rights may luff 'as she pleases', (ie as quickly as she likes) up to head-to-wind.

Rule 39.2 reads: 'After *starting* and clearing the starting line, subject to rule 32, a yacht *clear ahead* or a *leeward* yacht may *luff* as she pleases unless the *windward* yacht has been *mast abeam* at any time during the *overlap*.

It is important to bear in mind that a leeward yacht without luffing rights may luff to her proper course, but not as she pleases. She may only luff so as to allow her opponent an avenue of escape as she is subject to rule 35.

3. Luffing rights when starting

When the two yachts are overlapped at the moment that the leading yacht starts (ie first cuts the line after the starting signal), then the helmsmen (and umpires) need to assess whether, at that moment, the windward yacht is mast abeam. If there is reasonable doubt in the mind of the leeward yacht's helmsman, then a hail and hand signal by the windward yacht will be the determining factor. A wise helm of the windward yacht at or forward of mast abeam will always hail and signal as his yacht starts, and then for the duration of the overlap (if the yachts remain within two lengths of each other) the leeward yacht will not have luffing rights.

Should the windward yacht be abaft of mast abeam when the leading yacht starts (which is bound to be true on a square line if they both start at approximately the same time), then the leeward yacht will have luffing rights. However, although this gives her the right to luff head to wind, she has the right to luff 'as she pleases' only after she is clear of the starting line as this is when rule 39 takes over from rule 38.

LUFFING MATCH

The outcome of some matches result from a 'luffing match': a yacht tries to overtake close to windward to blanket the leeward yacht's wind, and the leeward yacht suddenly luffs. The leeward yacht tries to make contact before the windward yacht can reach the mast-abeam position resulting in a penalty being applied to the windward yacht for failing to keep clear; if the leeward yacht fails to make contact, the windward yacht will eventually take the leeward yacht's wind and therefore gain the lead.

As an alternative to trying to 'make contact', which could put her at risk should there be damage, the leeward yacht may luff and close the gap to such an extent that she could not luff further without making contact, thereby demonstrating that her luff has been curtailed by the windward yacht failing to keep clear. When the yachts are provided, and therefore only minor damage is required for there to be an infringement of rule 32, umpires should be more inclined to rule in favour of the leeward yacht.

HAILS AND HAILING (GENERAL)

A hail is a meaningful word or string of words, capable of being heard in the prevailing conditions. If Yellow hails and then claims that there was no response to her hail from Blue, or Blue claims that the hail was not heard , a protest committee would have to decide whether or not the hail has been properly made. They would consider: Were the words such that the meaning should have been understood? Was the hail loud enough to be heard in the prevailing conditions? Was it repeated?

Hails can be classified into three distinct types, and it is important to appreciate into which category each falls:

1. Provided they are not abusive or made with malicious intent, most hailed warnings and claims are usually of no significance. These include hails like 'I'm going to tack', 'I'm tacking', 'Starboard', 'Windward boat keep clear', 'Hold your course'. These are not really 'hails' in terms of the racing rules because there is no requirement to respond to them. Good match racing helmsmen rarely make such calls.

2. Hails of 'Water', 'No water', 'Overlap', 'No room' and 'No overlap' at a mark may have significance when they help to support a claim for room, although no longer mentioned in the rules. Such hails may therefore affect the actions of a yacht; but the hail itself does not place an obligation on the other yacht and is therefore of limited consequence.

3. Hails such as 'Water to tack' from a leeward, close hauled yacht approaching an obstruction; the reply of 'You tack'; and the hails of

'Mast abeam' and 'Obstruction (or similar)' from a windward yacht being luffed by a yacht to leeward, are all hails that have an important significance because in each case making the hail places an obligation on the other yacht which, without the hail she would not have. It follows that for the hail to be permitted, the hailing yacht must be in the relevant position. To make the hail when not in the relevant position is in itself an infringement.

To emphasise the difference between these hails, if a yacht hails 'Water' near a mark because she believes she has the right to room, then there is no obligation for the outside yacht to give room, and thus making the hail is not an infringement. However, if a yacht hails 'Water to tack' when there is no reason to believe that there is an obstruction ahead, or a yacht hails 'Mast abeam' when she is abaft the mast abeam position, then by making the hail, the yacht infringes a rule and a protest by the other yacht will be upheld.

When umpiring is being used, the hails of 'Mast abeam', 'Room to tack' and 'You tack' must be accompanied by the prescribed hand signal. Umpires will determine whether or not a hail of 'Mast-abeam' or 'Room to tack' is permitted, based upon the position of the yacht at the time the hand signal is made. When we refer to 'hail' throughout the book we include the required hand signal unless specified otherwise.

To hail and not signal may be taken as an attempt to cause your opponent to take action unnecessarily and without risk of penalty from the umpires for an unjustified hail. To signal and not hail may be taken to be an attempt to get a judgement from the umpires without giving your opponent the opportunity to respond. Either should be classed as unsportsmanlike behaviour and penalised accordingly.

HAILING FOR WATER AT A MARK, AND REPLYING

When umpiring is not being used, a crew member on the bow of Yellow with an inside overlap, other than one that is indisputable, should hail something like 'I have an overlap' before reaching the two length circle. If the outside yacht, Blue, hails something indicating agreement, then Yellow can assume she has the right to round inside. If Blue subsequently claims that the overlap is broken at the two length circle, she will be burdened with the onus of satisfying the protest committee that she broke the overlap, if there is a dispute.

If Blue does not respond to the hail by Yellow and there is a dispute, Blue will have weakened her case by not responding.

In match racing when umpiring is being used, there is no point in making hails of 'Room' or 'Water' at a mark because a wise skipper in the yacht ahead/outside will give no reply as he has no case to weaken.

HAILING 'MAST ABEAM'

A claim that a hail of 'Mast abeam' was improper cannot be judged by on-the-water umpires if they didn't hear the hail. For this reason the match racing appendix, when umpires are used, requires that the hail is accompanied by a hand signal: the helmsman repeatedly and conspicuously pointing towards the foot of the leeward yacht's mainmast. Umpires will assume that the hail is made simultaneously with the hand signal.

The effect of the hail and signal is that, when there is doubt, the luffing rights of the leeward yacht are removed, and her only remedy is to protest. The umpires will adopt the principle of wanting to be sure there was an infringement before imposing a penalty so a marginally early call will probably escape penalty. Be that as it may, there are two good reasons why the hail should not be made prematurely. First, because to do so knowingly is cheating, and secondly, umpires soon get to know that a particular competitor habitually hails early and that at some critical stage in a series, they may well uphold a protest and impose a penalty.

The response to a hail of 'Mast abeam' must be prompt. It cannot be delayed, nor may it be unduly slow. The windward yacht remains obliged to keep clear.

SLOWLY (RELATING TO RULE 38.2 - SAME TACK, AND LUFFING BEFORE CLEARING THE STARTING LINE)

When Yellow is either leeward yacht or clear ahead and luffs in such a way that Blue to windward or clear astern has to alter course to keep clear, any luff by Yellow must be 'slow'. We have often been asked 'How slow is slow?'. Although it is impossible to give a definitive answer, it should be borne in mind that a luff that was 'not fast' does not necessarily mean that it was 'slow'. When umpires are addressing whether a luff was 'slow', they must not be questioning whether or not the luff was fast and deducing that if it wasn't, the yacht didn't infringe. They should ask themselves, 'Was that luff slow?' and only if the answer is 'Yes' would the yacht satisfy the requirement. Of course, in keeping with the general policy of umpires penalising only when they are certain that there is an infringement, umpires will not penalise when in doubt, but if each of the two umpires is of the opinion that the luff was not slow (and the other yacht did have to alter course to keep clear) then they must penalise Yellow if there is a protest from Blue.

Perhaps it would be helpful to use three grades when talking about the speed of a luff: slow, medium and fast. Then it might be that a luff that is not fast or medium must indeed be slow.

INITIALLY

The word 'initially' appears twice in the racing rules. Rule 37.3 Transitional reads: 'A yacht that establishes an *overlap* to *leeward* from *clear astern* shall 'initially' allow the *windward* yacht ample room and opportunity to keep clear.' This means that there is a period of time, starting when the overlap is first established, after which the obligation to give ample room and opportunity ceases to exist. In making a decision as to whether contact occurred as a result of either:

- the leeward yacht not giving 'ample room and opportunity', or

- because the windward yacht did not take action to keep clear,

umpires will take into account what action the windward yacht has taken since the overlap was first established. If during this 'initial' period the windward yacht has taken no action (long enough for an umpire to say and repeat 'I've taken no action'), there is no obligation on the leeward yacht to give any further room or opportunity to the windward yacht to keep clear. The issue would depend upon any luff complying with the appropriate pre or post start limitations.

Umpires will agree the point in time when the overlap is established and monitor whether avoiding action by the windward yacht starts at that time. If it was prompt, any decision will favour the windward yacht and, if not, the leeward yacht.

The other place where the word 'initially' occurs is in rule 38.2 (Same tack - Luffing Before Clearing The Starting Line): Before she *starts* and clears the starting line, when a *leeward* yacht or a yacht *clear ahead luffs* so that another yacht will have to alter course to keep clear, she shall *luff* only slowly, and initially in such a way as to give the *windward* yacht room and opportunity to keep clear'.

The effect of the word 'initially' in this rule is seldom appreciated. It refers to the process of luffing. The 'initial' part of any change of course to windward must be such as to give a windward yacht room and opportunity to keep clear. If a leeward yacht luffs a little, then holds her course, then luffs again, both her luffs must comply with this requirement. However, there is a flaw in the wording of the rule. The windward yacht might have placed herself so close to the leeward yacht that any luff by the leeward yacht would result in contact. No luff could be 'in such a way as to give a windward yacht room and oppotunity to keep clear'.

In practice umpires will not penalise a leeward yacht luffing slowly into a windward yacht that has placed herself so perilously close. Since there is always the all-encompassing obligation on the leeward yacht to luff slowly it follows that if the windward yacht remains a sensible distance the 'room and opportunity' obligation tends to be automatically complied with. If not, was the windward yacht keeping clear, even before the luff? It would therefore be inadvisable for a windward yacht to rely on using the tactic of sailing so close to a leeward yacht that any luff by her would cause a collision.

COVERING

A leading yacht is said to be covering a trailing yacht when she responds to the escape attempts of the latter in order that she maintains control. This is generally achieved by remaining between your opponent and the next mark.

FREE LEG OF THE COURSE

The phrase 'on a free leg of the course' is used to determine when rules 39.3 (Sailing Below a Proper Course) and 54.3(b) (Pumping) apply. It is not a well chosen phrase for it implies that a leg of the course is either 'free' or it is not 'free'. Consider the following situations:

- a yacht sails significantly over the layline to the windward mark and then has to ease sails and reach to the mark.

- a yacht sails up the beat some way, tacking a few times, and then there is a significant windshift. She sails the remainder of the leg with spinnaker set.

- Although unlikely in match racing (unless one counts the close finishes in the 1990 Round the World Race as match racing), suppose a leg of a course is set such that there is a land mass between two successive marks. The yachts beat to a headland of the land mass and then bear away onto a reach to the next mark of the course.

It can only be that 'on a free leg of the course' means 'when the *current* proper course of a yacht requires her to be sailing free'. Thus a yacht that has sailed significantly over the layline will not be on a free leg until she has tacked for the mark. Until the tack she is not subject to rule 39.3 and may sail below her proper course without infringing, even to prevent a leeward yacht from making room to tack by bearing away (always providing she keeps clear).

BEATING TO WINDWARD

Whether a yacht is 'beating to windward' or not determines the type of exoneration she must complete if she is penalised. A yacht is beating to windward when her proper course is close hauled or she will have to tack prior to rounding the next mark of the course.

Interestingly, although the two expressions are not linked in the rules a yacht 'beating to windward' is not on a 'free leg'.

DAMAGE

When the yachts are provided by the organising authority rule 32 is amended by Appendix B6 to say 'A yacht shall attempt to avoid a collision resulting in damage'. Very laudable, but how do we decide what is damage and what is not?

It will be useful first to consider 'serious damage' as IYRU case 36 gives some guidance. It says that when determining if damage is 'serious', consideration must be given to:

- the extent and cost of repair of the damage relative to the size of the yacht concerned,

- whether the damage markedly affected her speed and materially prejudiced her finishing position, and

- whether or not it was prudent or feasible for her to continue to race.

Clearly we can assume that the word 'serious' is omitted from the appendix rule in order that lesser damage is included. This is quite intentional in order to protect yachts provided by organisers and to prevent aggression from getting out of hand.

Equally clearly a superficial mark would not qualify as damage. The best definition we have produced to date is that; if a prudent owner would repair without delay, then the damage comes within the scope of the rule.

Damage would include for instance, gelcoat damage likely to allow water into the sub layers, almost any sail tear, any damage to rigging, and a bent toe rail when its attachment to the hull is affected. It would exclude a superficial scratch, or a slight bend to a toe rail with no other problems.

In order to use this rule it is important that the damage can be attributable, without doubt, to a particular incident. Umpires, crews and organisers should inspect the yachts at the beginning of a regatta and even record the condition on video to assess the starting condition of each yacht.

One concern that remains is injury to crew members. While some injuries might be included in 'affecting the speed of the yacht' the rules do not specifically address the issue. We would like to think that competitors and judges alike would include injury requiring treatment as 'damage'.

3
The umpiring system

The conventional protest system with its long hearings, and decisions that often overturned the result of the race, is replaced by a system in which umpires aboard fast runabouts decide protests in respect to the 'sailing rules' (Part IV and some of Part V of the racing rules). Umpires try to position themselves in the best place to make good decisions and respond within seconds to protests by yachts or, for certain Part V rules, their own observations. When they believe the protested yacht has infringed a rule they impose a penalty, such as a tack or a gybe which, while putting the infringer at a disadvantage, will not necessarily determine the match. Using this system, it is very unusual for the yacht that crosses the finishing line first not to be the winner.

History

Many clubs had tried on-the-water judging, but it was only after it was used at the Maxi World Match Racing Championship in Newport in June 1987 that Tom Ehman, one of the judges from that event, wrote an enthusiastic report which he presented to the IYRU Annual Conference in November of that year. The Judges Sub-committee of the Racing Rules Committee sanctioned an experimental phase, and the system was used and developed extensively during 1988 at most of the major match racing regattas. It is now inconceivable that umpiring will not be used at all major match racing regattas, including the America's Cup, the World Championship of Match Race Sailing, the IYRU Nations Cup, and the final parts of the Soling championships at the Olympics.

How it works

Two umpires in a fast manoeuvrable runabout closely watch the two yachts, positioning themselves in such a way that they can best judge an incident should one arise. When the two competing yachts are close to each other, the umpire boat will also be close to them. When the two yachts are well separated, the umpires will maintain a greater distance to reduce the possibility of interference. A second runabout called a 'wing boat' is often used at major events to radio or hand signal information about overlaps, mast beam positions and distance from marks to the umpires in order to help them make correct decisions. As an alternative to wing boats, an observer is placed on the stern of each yacht and communicates to the umpires with standard hand signals.

It is a fundamental principle that the umpires never impose a penalty on a yacht for infringing a right of way rule unless the other yacht has protested (displaying international code flag Y is the standard signal). Even if they see a collision and neither yacht protests the umpires will not initiate action themselves unless they believe there is a possibility of damage. Rule 33, Contact between Yachts Racing, and hence the mandatory requirement to protest, retire or take a penalty after a collision, is deleted with umpiring.

Another fundamental principle is that a skipper believing his yacht has infringed a rule is not required to take a penalty until and unless the umpires signal to him to take one; this is an important variation to fundamental rule D which normally requires a yacht realising she has infringed a rule to take the appropriate action.

A third fundamental principle is that umpires will not penalise a yacht unless they are satisfied that the yacht has infringed a rule. Even when there is contact, and both yachts protest, if the umpires cannot decide which yacht is at fault they will not penalise either yacht.

John well remembers his first ever 'call' as an umpire. The two yachts were approaching a port hand leeward mark on port tack, clearly overlapped and both with spinnakers flying. The outside yacht gave the required room, just, and both started to round, dropping kites at the same time. All was well until a crew member on the inside yacht detached the spinnaker halyard from the head of the sail and promptly let it go. The halyard swung outward and over a crewman of the outside yacht. Thinking that it must be his own yacht's halyard, he smartly grabbed hold and attached it to the lifelines! The two yachts then proceeded, attached, upwind, each displaying a protest flag. After some discussion on the umpire boat, but with no conclusion, neither yacht was penalised. (He still doesn't know which yacht infringed!)

Equipment needed for competitors

Each yacht is provided with an international code flag Y which is the standard protest flag for signalling a protest to be decided by the umpires during the race. The Y flag should measure about 1 ft (300 mm) on the hoist and be fixed to a stick about 3 ft (1 m) long. An 18 in (0.5 m) long, 2 in (5 cm) diameter, plastic tube can be attached to the pushpit. The stick is housed flag down in the tube. When the yacht wants to make the signal, a crew member simply pulls out the stick, turning it flag up, waves it, and places it in the tube with the flag flying. When the decision is given, the flag is withdrawn, turned upside down and replaced in the tube. On yachts without pushpits the crew need to work out a satisfactory place to keep the flag at the ready and simply wave it conspicuously when it is required.

A red international code flag B is usually also provided, often tied permanently to the backstay or shroud, and furled with a velcro strip. This is used for the type of protest or request for redress to be resolved after the race.

Frequently the yachts are provided by the organisers and then the sailing instructions normally call for a 'breakdown signal' (usually a white flag or code L meaning: 'I require the repair service and request a delay in the next starting sequence until I am fixed'). When assistance is required, the signal is made *between* races as a breakdown *during* a race is normally excluded in the sailing instructions as grounds for redress after the first warning signal of each race sequence.

Almost universal now is the identification of the yachts, within each pair, by the display of either a blue flag (port end assigned yacht) or yellow flag (starboard end assigned yacht). These flags, with a fly of approx 18 in (0.5 m), are best attached to sticks; these in turn are taped to the backstay as appropriate for each start. If this system is not used, then the yachts will need some other form of identification. At major regattas it is not uncommon for special new sails with the initials of the skippers, instead of sail numbers, to be provided.

Equipment needed for umpires

The best type of umpire boat depends to a large extent on the sea state. On flat water, this will be something like either a 16 ft (5 m) RIB (rigid bottomed, inflatable boat) or an 18 ft (6 m) whaler (dory in the UK) with at least a 60 hp outboard, with central console to stand behind and hold on to. In rougher waters, a larger RIB would suit most conditions. In heavy seas, sportsboats with twin drives, about 30 ft (10 m) long, with a single-storey flying bridge with plastic windows for protection from the spray and weather, have been used. However, the windage and wash they cause can be a problem. An experienced driver, in addition to the umpires, is essential in this type of boat.

The best crew for an umpire boat is either two or three people depending on whether separate drivers are used or not. The driver, umpire or not, must have the ability to manoeuvre at both high and low speed in close quarter situations and be able to anticipate the tactics the yachts will use. Most experienced umpires would rather drive themselves than have to cope with umpiring *and* directing an inexperienced driver. Sometimes an extra 'umpire' is on board to provide for some off-duty time or it may be someone wanting to gain experience. Extra people not only add weight, reduce manoeuvrability and increase wash but they can also detract from the job the umpires are there to do.

Wing boats need to be manoeuvrable and fast; they are therefore often small and, on all but the smoothest water, wet. An experienced driver is required together with a 'wing judge', and a radio link to the umpire boat. They may also be provided with a full set of umpire boat gear so that they are equipped to take over at a moment's notice if required.

These boats are the legs of the umpires, provide the protection from the elements for the umpires and hold all the umpires' equipment. If they are not up to the job the umpires will have difficulty doing a good job. (Organisers be warned!)

Each umpire boat is equipped with:

- identification flags, blue and yellow (or plaques) for the yachts

- a green flag

- a black flag

- a sound source for signals (referees' whistles are best)

- radios for communication with the race committee, other umpires and wing judges, on a different frequency from the race committee's working channel

- tape recorder (weatherproof!)

- sailing instructions - preferably in plastic wallets

- schedule of races - may be in the SIs but separate and waterproof is useful

Flags should be about 2 ft 6 in (80 cm) on the fly (yes, *that* large), attached to sticks. Half inch (15 mm) plastic tubing with corks in each end in order that they float make exceedingly cheap, durable, light and waterproof 'sticks'. The best material we have found to date for the flags is nylon parachute cloth. It is waterproof, brightly coloured and doesn't crackle like spinnaker cloth.

If identification plaques are used they should be at least 18 in (0.5 m) square, white with black lettering on both sides. Two letters to identify each skipper are needed if the focus is on the skippers, which is usually the case. For example, CD is used for Chris Dickson. If the focus is on nationality, then obviously letters identifying the country would be used ~ preferably the new three letter Olympic standard.

Whatever is used for umpires' signals the same should be used for the recall signals from the committee boat and to identify which yacht has won the match at the end.

When the blue/yellow system is used for signalling, the yachts will need individual identification for other purposes so that spectators, media and the race officials can ensure that the correct skippers are paired. This identification should be used on sails, dodgers, score sheets and everywhere the individuals need to be identified.

The sound source for signals has often been a problem. Some lower frequency horns cannot be heard over the noise of the wind in the rigging and sails flapping. Portable aerosol horns are rarely loud enough, frequently unreliable and difficult to stow safely yet be readily to hand. A top quality referee's whistle seems to be the best all round choice.

The radio link to the race committee needs to be portable, reliable, and usually in waterproof wallets specifically designed for the purpose. A speaker to enable both umpires to hear the calls from the wing boat is a useful addition. Cheap CB type radios just do not seem to be up to the job and all need large well charged battery packs if they are to last what are frequently long days.

Appointment and training of umpires

The knowledge and experience of umpires, like members of the protest committees, will depend largely on the importance of the event. Top events will use International Umpires appointed by the IYRU and National Umpires appointed by national authorities. Club events will include the use of local volunteers. Experienced sailors, especially experienced match race sailors, often make excellent umpires with little practice.

Whatever the event, a Chief Umpire should be appointed; usually he or she will double as chairman of the protest committee (or International Jury at an international event).

Typically the pairs of umpires will be so arranged that each of the less experienced will be partnered with one of the more experienced. All umpires should at some time work as a wing judge. During an event the pairs are changed on a daily basis in order to gain as much from each other as possible.

The International Umpires' scheme is administered by the International Yacht Racing Union (IYRU), and includes the publishing of and updating of an Umpires' Manual and the Umpires' Calls Book. In addition umpiring seminars are arranged around the world and are mandatory for International Umpires. National authorities are encouraged to develop National Umpire schemes. All of these developments strive towards providing a first class service for competitors and for the sport, with decisions that are correct and judgements that are consistent.

Operation of the umpire pair

The umpires decide who is to monitor each of the two yachts, usually standing either side of the centre console. With the umpire's boat heading into the wind the umpire standing on the port side might 'adopt' the yacht entering the starting area from the port end (blue in the blue/yellow system), and have 'his' yacht's flag or placard near to him. In this book, when we refer to 'Yellow's umpire' or 'Blue's umpire', we don't mean that Yellow or Blue has their own umpire; we refer to the umpire who, it has been decided, will monitor that particular yacht.

The umpires then:

- identify the moment when the yachts assume a collision course, and the moment at which there is a change of relationship (eg a new overlap, or one of the yachts completes a tack, or when they have reached the point at which they are about to round a mark, and so on)
- decide which is the 'right-of-way' yacht and why
- decide what are the obligations of each yacht (e.g. keep clear, or give room, or tack etc)
- decide whether each yacht is fulfilling her obligations
- anticipate what is likely to happen and discuss the implications.

Each umpire speaks aloud as 'his' yacht changes its relationship with the other, or changes its own status. Each speaks as things happen, without worrying about interupting his partner. One might say 'Tack complete, I am right of way, starboard'. He hears his partner say 'I am give way, port, I am tacking, tack complete, right of way, clear ahead' while he continues with 'I am give way, clear astern'.

This commentary continues while the two yachts are near each other with the possibility of interaction, which in the pre-start might be most of the time, but after the start is likely to be less frequent. The umpires will also check with each other on any issues that may arise. For example, as yachts approach an obstruction, they will agree on the point at which an overlap will be necessary for one yacht to have the right to room, or whether it is relevant if a yacht is sailing her proper course.

Operation of the wing boat

We have yet to meet a wing boat judge who has not succumbed to the temptation to make a call when he is not in the correct position, including ourselves. Knowing that the umpires are hungry for the knowledge as to whether or not there is, for example, an overlap, the wing judge will make a judgement even though he is out of position, and radio the message 'Negative overlap' or 'Overlap', or whatever.

It takes experience to learn that it is just not possible to tell unless you are 'lined up', no matter how obvious it may seem; and if it is really obvious, then the umpires can see for themselves anyway.

What is worse, if you do it too often, at some time the umpires will be in a perfect position to be absolutely certain that you are wrong. The confidence they have in all your calls from then on will inevitably be reduced, sometimes to the point of being ignored.

Figs 23a to h give a general guide to the positioning of umpire and wing judge boats. In general during the pre-start manoeuvres, when the umpires trail 'the gap' between the two competing yachts, the information they will want is whether or not an overlap exists, and whether or not the windward yacht is mast abeam. In the pre-start period, when rights and obligations change as these two relationships alter, it is often difficult for the umpire boat and the wing judge boat to maintain good positions and avoid interfering with the match.

It is worth remembering while trying to do so that there are relatively few incidents while the yachts are actually circling, but more when they break away and most of all when one yacht is on the other's tail. Being in a postion to anticipate and respond to the break away is therefore relatively more important than the 'model' position while circling.

Suppose both yachts circle an obstruction, the committee boat for instance; if they are close together the umpire boat should follow them round, but if they are well apart it is best to remain to leeward of the obstruction moving to one side or other depending on which side the yachts approach each other closest.

On-board observers

The Royal New Zealand Yacht Squadron provided on-board observers for the World Match Racing Championships in November

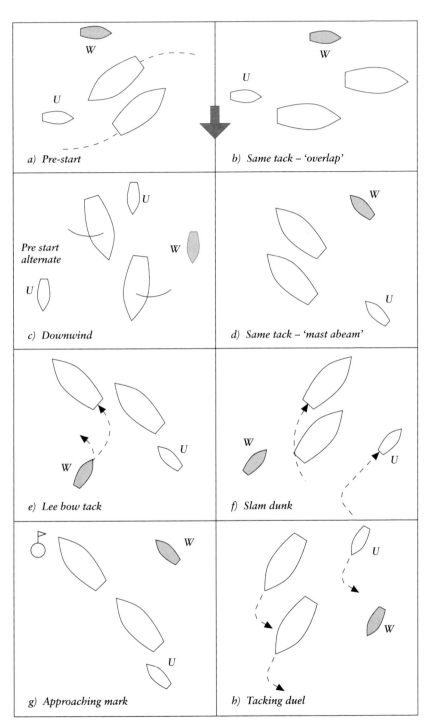

a) Pre-start

b) Same tack – 'overlap'

Pre start alternate

c) Downwind

d) Same tack – 'mast abeam'

e) Lee bow tack

f) Slam dunk

g) Approaching mark

h) Tacking duel

FIG 23: POSITIONING OF UMPIRE AND WING BOATS

1990 as has the Royal Lymington Yacht Club for the Royal Lymington Cup from 1991 onwards. Shortly before the preparatory signal, an observer is put aboard each yacht, having previously been weight equalised; this person stands on either special foot platforms or the yacht's scoop stern and holds on to the pushpit framework. In New Zealand their role was to signal overlaps and contact while in Lymington their role has been extended to include mast abeam (achieved by the addition of tape stripes on the hulls of the yachts; these are the same distance back from the mast as the observer is back from the skipper in an agreed 'normal position').

The signals are arm-up for overlap or mast abeam and arm-out for no overlap or no mast abeam, it should be obvious which is being signalled. Contact is signalled by a head-pat. The system has the following advantages over wing boats:

- the observers are always in the correct position leading to better calls
- there is a reduced requirement for umpire boats and their associated fuel and berthing facilities
- the umpires have an immediate independent contact on the boat to assess what help is needed for breakdowns, which is sometimes vital to the timely progress of the regatta
- the observers are in a good position to be independent witnesses for protests regarding the rules of inspection.

Change in tactics

When umpires are used, the tactics of the competitors need to be different. In high profile competitions like the America's Cup where no expense is spared, aggressive tactical scenarios were developed, but their success depended in part on the presentation in the jury room. As rules adviser to the Swedish team in 1980, the British Victory syndicate in 1983 and the Australian Kookaburra syndicate in 1986-7, Bryan developed many ideas for getting 'a kill' on the water, as an alternative to winning with superior boat speed. However, they depended as much on opportunity as skill of execution, and needed an elaborate array of evidence collecting equipment to portray the incident accurately in the jury room.

Often the jury would not readily accept a particular interpretation. In 1983, one of *Victory's* protests revolved around whether she had delayed changing course when faced with her opponent who had just tacked on to starboard. It was obvious that one of the jury members was of the opinion that *Victory* should have anticipated becoming the give way yacht and have begun to keep clear before her opponent had completed her tack to starboard. Although the theme of anticipation is fundamental to good seamanship and a cornerstone of the International Regulations for the Preventing of Collisions at Sea (IRPCAS), no such obligation exists in the racing rules. In this particular case, the other jury members were able to convince the jury member that he was wrong but it took time and discussion to do so. Had that jury member been the one on the water acting as an umpire, there would have been no such opportunity.

Thus one of the differences is that skippers and tacticians need to be aware that umpires can only judge what they see in relation to what they know; there is no opportunity for argument. Dennis Conner and his tactician Tom Whidden, after the spectacular Conner/Murray re-run of the 1987 America's Cup in the two *Kookaburras* in Sydney Harbour in January 1989, asked if it would be possible to have a radio link between the yachts and the umpires so that they could explain what they were protesting about. Though such a system would be possible, it would not necessarily be practical, and most would agree it would be undesirable. When umpires are used, the game changes and the opportunities for complex and clever tactical manoeuvres designed to be won in the protest room become a phenomenon of the past. This is no bad thing.

The other main difference of attitude by the wise skipper is in what he thinks about immediately after an incident. With conventional hearings, it is important to spend some time memorising what happened so that when asked to recall events many hours later in the jury room, a logical account can be given. When umpires are used and a decision to penalise is given, the wise skipper of the penalised yacht will think only of how to minimise the effect of the penalty, and how to get back into the race. Any skipper who wastes time and effort on cursing the umpires, or telling his crew that the decision was wrong, is simply adding to the effect of the penalty.

Penalties with umpiring

The advent of umpiring could have occurred without changing the basic penalty of disqualification. The match results would still be decided on the water and all those tedious hearings avoided. However, the emphasis would have firmly remained on causing your opponent to infringe. Reducing the penalty, to such an extent that the match is not lost, has brought into balance the other skills of sailing and hence vastly increased the interest in the game.

When developing the alternatives the objective has been that the penalty should be sufficient to ensure that the infringing yacht loses control of the match (normally two to three boat lengths) without, as far as possible, inevitably determining the outcome. It is, however, a fact that no matter how small the penalty, if it occurs close enough to the finishing line it will determine the match. It is also a fact that any penalty requiring a yacht to do something will have varying effect, depending upon the type of yacht, the sails she has set at the time, her point of sailing, the wind and the sea conditions.

It is for these reasons that the appendix specifically states, 'The sailing instructions may prescribe different penalties'. The organisers should consider this carefully, especially if they are using yachts different in nature to those more commonly used. Careful thought and talking to experienced umpires and competitors will help in this area.

Penalties of Appendix B6

What is the penalty? The penalty to be taken is determined by when the penalty is signalled. It is not determined by when the incident took place.

First the yacht must 'sail clear of the other yacht' and either,

- 'When beating to windward, the penalty shall be a gybe', or

- 'When not beating to windward, the penalty shall be a tack'.

If you have to do more than one gybe penalty, as would be the case when penalised twice during the pre-start period, you must luff to a close hauled course in between each. This piece of fine tuning came in to prevent a yacht, penalised a number of times, from bearing away to dead downwind, hauling in the mainboom almost to the centreline and then merely flicking it and the sail across as many times as there were penalties to be taken, thus effectively negating all but the first penalty.

When must the penalty be taken? Again the time of signalling the penalty determines when the penalty must be taken:

- 'when the penalty is signalled before she has started, it shall be taken as soon as possible after starting'

- 'when the penalty is signalled after she has started, it shall be taken as soon as possible, except that when the head of her spinnaker is above the main boom gooseneck the penalty may be taken at any time on that leg of the course provided that the spinnaker is first lowered so that its head is below the gooseneck and remains so until the tack is completed.'

So, there are two circumstances when the penalty must be delayed, but what is 'as soon as possible' and what defines 'the leg of the course'?

'As soon as possible' will allow a yacht to sail on to ensure that while completing her penalty she will not foul another yacht or obstruction. The penalty is never intended to be larger than prescribed by virtue of the proximity of the committee boat or a spectator vessel, for instance. In practice, the umpire of the penalised yacht should be saying 'I can't take it yet I'd hit the committee boat... I could clear it now...I must now take my penalty... If I don't do it now I'm going to get another penalty... do you agree? (to his fellow umpire)' and if the exoneration is not initiated the umpires will use their power to impose a further, 'umpire initiated penalty'.

The leg of the course is the one on which the penalty is signalled. In order to prevent a yacht from largely negating the penalty by tacking round a leeward mark, the end of the leg is set as an imaginary line from the previous mark and projected through the mark being rounded.

Umpires should refrain from signalling penalties whenever it might cause confusion as to what penalty the yacht should take. For example, a yacht infringing with a late lee-bow tack approaching the windward mark might well have her penalty signalled soon after clearing the mark, although in fact the umpires may have decided the issue some seconds earlier.

Penalties initiated by umpires

Previously, at the beginning of this section, we said that umpires never impose a penalty for an infringement of the right of way rules unless there has been a protest. This is true, but there are some other rules, infringements of which Appendix B6 specifically requires the umpires to act with an 'umpire initiated penalty'. In all these cases competitors are excluded from protesting, and therefore the burden for ensuring compliance rests solely with the umpires. The specific rules to which these apply are:

- rule 52, Touching a Mark
- rule 54, Propulsion
- Appendix B6 para 4, Pre-start and Starting Requirements
- Appendix B6 para 5.3, 5.5 and 5.6, Penalties
- breach of good sportsmanship.

In all these cases the penalty is exactly the same as described above.

In very specific circumstances the umpires may also impose a 'black flag' penalty: instant disqualification, but this is limited to:

- a yacht that does not take a penalty as signalled

- a yacht that gains an advantage from infringing despite having taken a penalty

- as a possible alternative to the normal penalty in the case of a breach of good sportsmanship.

There are no circumstances when the umpires are compelled to use the black flag, they always have the alternative of a further 'tack or gybe' penalty, which should be used in all but the most extreme cases.

Time penalties

At the 1991 Royal Lymington Cup a new approach to on-the-water penalties was tested: time penalties. Instead of being required to 'do a penalty' the umpires kept score of the penalty tally in each match. Each penalty was worth 'one unit' of time, which was set by the race committee at the start to equal three to four boat lengths in the prevailing conditions (normally 15, 20 or 25 seconds increasing as the winds became lighter).

The umpires were empowered to give additional penalties if they felt that the infringement would result in a significant advantage. There was a back stop built in so that if one yacht at any time carried three more units of penalty than her opponent, she would be automatically disqualified.

Towards the end of the race the umpires would radio the committee boat to let them know the number of units *difference* between the two yachts and which one the penalty was to be applied to. For the spectators, the CB displayed a large board with the number of seconds within which the second boat must finish of the first in order to win the match (the other way round, the penalty is irrelevant anyway). As the second boat finished the CB would display the blue or yellow flag of the winner. It was surprisingly exciting to watch even though the principle of first across the line wins was sacrificed.

The system has three major advantages:

- the penalty is varied to have the same effect no matter what the conditions

- it is independent of where on the course the infringement occurs

- it keeps the yachts together on the race course.

The major disadvantage that a penalised yacht remains able to control the race was largely overcome by a modification to the system in 1992. For one pre-start infringement the penalised yacht was required to cross the transom of her opponent. This worked well and may be considered as an alternative to the conventional tack or gybe.

Hitting marks

As stated earlier, when we listed the rules that changed with umpiring, rule 52.2, Exoneration after Touching a Mark, is deleted so that the penalties become the same as any other umpire initiated penalty. It is worth while spending a few moments to clarify the implications of this change.

First, the rule that prohibits a yacht from touching marks (rule 52.1) remains, and it is only the exoneration that has changed. No longer do you have to do a 360 degree turn but you do the same penalty as for any other on-the-water penalty.

This means that, when penalised by the umpires, if you hit a starting mark before starting you must delay your penalty until after starting, unlike the normal rule which requires you to take the penalty as soon as possible.

Should you hit a finishing mark, then you have not finished until you have completed the penalty, returned wholly to the course side of the finishing line, and then crossed the finishing line in accordance with the definition. Hitting a finishing mark is the one time when you might be wise to take your penalty before the umpire's signal. Imagine that you hit the mark and your opponent is four boat lengths behind. You have a reasonable chance of completing the penalty and still winning the match. On the other hand, if you wait for the umpires to decide (they must talk to each other and agree to penalise) and then signal the penalty, your opponent has probably long finished, while you are by now a long way from the finishing line.

If the match is so close that taking the penalty will cost you a win, then you should wait and hope.

Should you touch a mark but believe that it was only as a result of being 'wrongfully compelled' (as rule 52.3 says) to do so by another yacht, then you must protest to avoid penalty. Rule 52.3 still applies and allows exoneration as does the match racing appendix. The umpires would need to be sure that the one was as a direct consequence of the other, and of course if the other yacht is not penalised then you most certainly will be, even without protest from the other yacht.

4
The pre-start
(The preparatory period)

The preparatory period is the period between the preparatory signal and the starting signal, usually 4 or 5 minutes, but it is mostly referred to as 'the pre-start'.

However, this chapter will deal with tactics and situations not up to the starting signal, but only up to the point at which yachts might approach the line to start. Chapter 5 will deal with the period around the time of the starting signal.

Manoeuvring in this period can often provide an opportunity for gaining a substantial advantage for one yacht over her opponent and is the period where match racing differs most from fleet racing.

Without the system of umpiring, a match can be won in the pre-start period simply by having an incident and winning the resulting protest after the match. If there is a collision, the resulting protest would invariably determine the result of the match, since one yacht has to be disqualified, and which yacht crossed the finishing line first would be irrelevant. Thus a skipper who believes he has the slower yacht might decide that his best chance of victory is to cause an infringement by his opponent in the pre-start period; the skipper believing he has a faster yacht might try to avoid interacting and thereby reduce the chance of infringement.

Even with the use of umpires, a yacht causing her opponent to infringe a rule will gain a significant advantage by the opponent being penalised. As the penalty has to be taken after starting, the 'winner' of the incident will gain two or three boat lengths' advantage. When a penalty is awarded in the pre-start, the yachts continue to manoeuvre against each other.

General strategy during the pre-start

There are two principal objectives during the pre-start manoeuvring. The first is to be in a position to 'win the start' and the second is to have a penalty advantage over your opponent. Which is more important depends upon many factors; these will be discussed as we go through the various options.

It follows that well before the preparatory signal you need to have decided to what extent you are going to do battle with your opponent and what your ideal start will be, at least in terms of port/starboard end, windward/leeward position, and port/starboard tack. Many skippers when they start match racing forget all about race strategy in favour of boat-to-boat battles and unnecessarily lose a lot of matches. Having decided your pre-start objectives, on with the race!

The first step, to avoid an umpire initiated penalty, is to fulfil the 'pre-start requirement' of Appendix B6, para 3. Unless amended by the sailing instructions, this requires you to be 'outside' your assigned end at the preparatory signal, and to first cross and clear the starting line from the course side within the next 2 minutes.

'Outside' means outside a line drawn at right angles to the starting line, through the end of the starting line. Note that this is different from the triangle typically used in fleet racing to control premature starters. This is deliberate as it avoids giving one yacht an advantage when the windward mark is offset to allow for tide or currents.

It is wise to enter the area within a few seconds of the preparatory signal, because your opponent, having fulfilled the entry requirements, is permitted to manoeuvre against you to keep you from doing so, resulting in penalty. Also, the earlier you are the more time you will have to initiate your own plan for the pre-start.

If you have decided you will be faster after the start and weaker in the pre-start battles, you will want to stay out of trouble and concentrate on the actual start. So, after entering from the right (looking in the direction of the course) on starboard tack you will gybe immediately around the starting mark (normally the committee boat) to head off on a port reach. When entering from the left you will sail straight at your opponent, changing course to keep clear at the last moment (so he cannot manoeuvre against you) and sail away, again reaching on port, before returning to approach the line on starboard. You will also need to keep an eye on the clock in order to properly time your run.

If you have decided you are superior in the pre-start battles (or not prepared to admit otherwise!), then you will do battle with your opponent. Initially the emphasis is on trying to get him to infringe a rule, while not infringing yourself, but later the emphasis shifts towards achieving the chosen start and being 'in control'.

The best you could achieve might be: one or possibly two penalties on your opponent, then forcing him over the line early such that he also hits the mark while you are one second behind the line, at your chosen end, sailing at full speed, against Peter Gilmour. Such are the dreams of match race skippers!

Should you achieve a penalty on your opponent you might well review your strategy. To continue to do battle will carry the risk of an equalising penalty on you or, as you now know that the other yacht will have to complete a penalty gybe soon after starting, your ideal start may well need modifying to ensure you are 'in control' with the minimum of post start manoeuvring. If you can start just to leeward, your opponent will have to tack away before being able to gybe. This effectively increases his penalty and ensures your control afterwards.

Unfortunately, of course, should *you* be the one penalised the same review will need to take place, but in reverse. All is not lost though, as you may achieve that equalising penalty or be able to force him over the line at the start.

The safe triangle and critical areas behind the starting line

Fig 24 shows the starting line, and various imaginary areas formed by the laylines to the ends of the starting line.

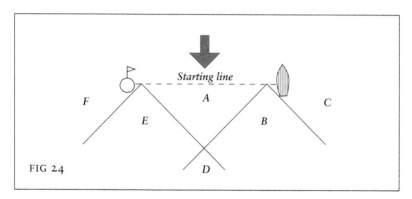

FIG 24

It is essential to know throughout the preparatory period what area you are in, or approaching, in relation to the time remaining to the starting signal.

Area A is known as the 'safe triangle', simply because when you are in this area it is very difficult for your opponent to stop you starting. However, as the starting signal is getting close, a leeward yacht may try to force a windward yacht over the line; a windward yacht will be trying to ensure that the leeward yacht starts in dirty air and certainly not in the safe lee-bow position (Fig 20).

Area B is reasonably safe; a yacht being chased there, while on port tack, will need little room to be able to gybe on to starboard, luff and head back into the safe triangle.

Area C is safe enough provided that you have time to gybe round and return to the triangle. However, it is not so safe if you are the windward of your pair and time is running short.

Area D is not so desirable if your opponent is between you and the line. You can only get back into the safe triangle by first passing through either E or B. To get to B you have to risk sailing on port, and we talk about E next.

Area E spells danger for a yacht being chased. If she bears away to gybe, a skilled opponent can bear away too and prevent the gybe; if the chased yacht tries to tack, the controlling yacht luffs to prevent her. The real danger is that, whichever way she goes, the chased yacht has to become the give way yacht, either port or tacking and therefore in trouble.

Area F, the red zone, is without doubt the most dangerous of all. Even if the chased boat manages to tack, she is still in trouble as she will be luffed the wrong side of the line by the controlling yacht who will easily start correctly herself.

It can be appreciated that there is a significant difference between 'going right' where the chased yacht can so easily gybe on to starboard to return to the safe middle area, and 'going left' where the gybe onto port tack can often be prevented by the controlling yacht on starboard tack.

Having said all this, it takes considerable skill and practice to trap an opponent to the left, and even against skilled opposition a yacht can often escape by using an obstruction such as a spectator boat (described later in this chapter). However, it is useful to be aware of the significance of the areas, and develop a game plan of at least trying to trap one's opponent to the left while avoiding being trapped there oneself. An alternative is to trap an opponent to windward, in the area off the starboard quarter of the committee boat (*area C*) shortly before the starting gun.

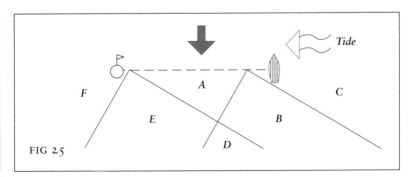

FIG 25

Fig 25 shows the effect of a cross tide, distorting the area shapes. Notice how a left-going tidal stream enlarges the danger areas E and F, and whichever way the stream is going, except with the wind, the size of the safe area will be reduced.

Manoeuvring against a give way yacht; rule 35 (Modified by Appendix B6 para 1.2)

This first scenario is frequently seen at the beginning of the match, when the two yachts first approach each other. It is fundamentally important because it shows how rule 35 is interpreted (Fig 26).

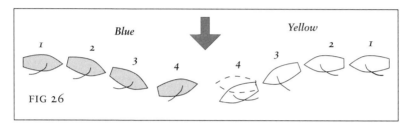

FIG 26

Blue enters from the port end and Yellow from the starboard end. At position 1 they are on a collision course. However, umpires would say to one another as they watched the two opponents approach each other, that there is 'no issue' yet; that is, Blue is not obliged, at that moment in time, to take any avoiding action.

This is an important point; Blue is, of course, required to 'keep clear', but continuing to sail a course that is or may be a collision course is not in itself an infringement. Because of the large distance between the two yachts, Blue is 'keeping clear'.

At position 2, Blue decides to bear away; Yellow continues on a steady course. They are no longer on a collision course and Blue is 'keeping clear'.

Now at position 3, Yellow bears away onto a collision course. Has she infringed rule 35? Has she obstructed Blue? The answer is, most definitely, no. Blue has ample opportunity to keep clear, either by luffing and passing to windward, or bearing away and passing to leeward or, for that matter, tacking or gybing.

At position 3 there is still no requirement for Blue to change course because she would be able to continue for at least another boat length and still keep clear without difficulty.

Position 4 represents a special moment; Blue must now do something. Yellow may have set her course so that Blue only has one option; in this case to luff. That is OK. Provided Yellow leaves at least one option open that Blue can take in a seamanlike manner,

Yellow does not infringe rule 35. The precise distance between the boats at this special moment will vary, to some extent, with the prevailing conditions and the type of yachts.

Had Yellow luffed at position 4 (dotted outline), it may have been impossible or difficult for Blue to keep clear whatever she did; then Yellow would have infringed rule 35, and if Blue were to protest, the umpires would penalise Yellow. Blue should still do what she is able to in order to avoid contact. Shouting 'hold your course' but doing nothing to try to keep clear will put Blue at great risk.

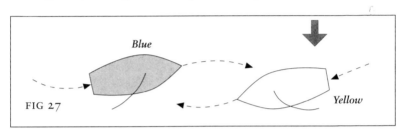

FIG 27

In Fig 27, which starts at position 4 from Fig 26, Blue has taken the option left open to her and has kept clear by luffing.

Now there is nothing to oblige Yellow to hold her course. As in Fig 26, Yellow may luff so as to get close to Blue's starboard quarter, perhaps in preparation for a turn around Blue's stern. Blue must respond to the luff by Yellow as much as she is able, however, she is not required to attempt to tack at this stage. Yellow must permit Blue to pass to windward.

Thus the two circle, each hoping to turn more tightly than her opponent, come out on her opponent's tail, and commence chasing, worrying and possibly controlling her.

Although this opening manoeuvre, where the yachts circle, each trying to get on to the tail of her opponent, is common, it is rare for either yacht to infringe a rule. Rule 35 ensures that the give way yacht is protected while the right of way yacht is continually altering course, providing the give way yacht continues to do her best to keep clear.

Reaching to the left

In Fig 28, Yellow has successfully 'got on the tail' of Blue who is heading off on starboard tack to the left hand side, into area E and possibly F, the red zone! (See Fig 25.)

As Blue bears away with the hope of gybing and then returning to safety, Yellow also bears away and is clearly able to prevent the gybe, providing she can achieve position 3 in Fig 28. Should Blue manage to gybe she will soon be forced back on to starboard.

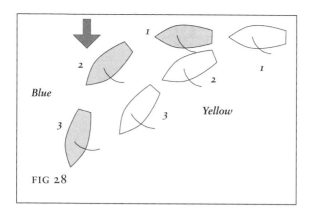

FIG 28

However, achieving position Yellow 3 is not quite so easy as it first appears. You will notice that Yellow has to turn more tightly than Blue and also with less speed (the distance between positions 1 and 2, and 2 and 3 is smaller for Yellow).

If Yellow turns more tightly with the same speed or greater she will soon be well overlapped to leeward. This will give Blue the opportunity to escape by luffing hard and tacking. If she falls too far behind then Blue will succeed in gybing away to safety. At position 2, Blue changes from the right of way yacht (clear ahead) to the give way yacht (windward), a point in time that must be recognised by crew and umpires alike.

In Fig 29, which starts from the same position as Fig 28 with Yellow on the tail of Blue, Blue chooses to luff in the hope of tacking. Yellow responds by also luffing; clearly, Blue would infringe were she to tack from position 4. (Don't forget that the tack does not start until Blue is beyond head-to-wind, until then, she is luffing.)

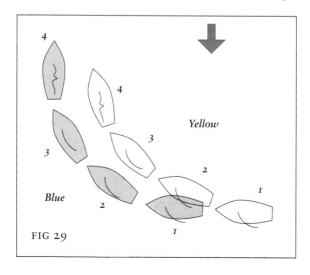

FIG 29

Again Yellow has to turn more tightly and must travel more slowly so that she is always in a position to bear away again should Blue do so. This situation, although it has some similarities with the one above, is different for two very important reasons. First, Blue is luffing, not bearing away, and that means rule 38 comes into effect. If Yellow has to respond in order to avoid a collision Blue may only luff slowly. Yellow remains the give way yacht throughout - first, 'clear astern', then 'windward'. Unless Blue goes beyond head-to-wind to become the give way yacht, rule 35 never applies to Yellow.

So, even 'simple' scenarios have complexities that need to be learned before going racing. The whole crew of a match racing team need to understand these, for controlling a yacht with this degree of accuracy requires precise sail handling as well as accurate helming. If the skipper has to take time to give instructions, to ease or pull sheets, the opponent will not only be off the hook but the stranglehold will soon be reversed.

Blue must realise the difficulties she can cause Yellow, just by altering course. She should do so and be prepared for any opportunity to escape. The route least likely to catch Yellow out is a steady, rythmical series of luffs and bear aways. Far more likely to work is to sail a while then suddenly turn one way or the other, sometimes slowly, sometimes fast (when the rules allow), sometimes going head-to-wind and holding for a time. Try something, doing nothing is just what Yellow wants to make life easy.

What else can Blue do to escape? Well, for one thing, she can look out for other types of opportunities to help her out. The classic is the 'spectator boat', mark laying boat or any other object that can be used as an obstruction.

Fig 30, from which Yellow has been omitted for clarity, shows Blue, clear ahead, passing close to leeward of the moored vessel, luffing immediately to close hauled, tacking as soon as she is able to clear the anchor line and off to the safe triangle. There is little Yellow

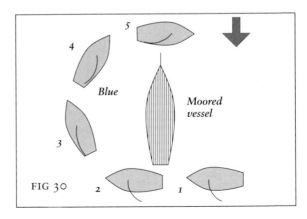

FIG 30

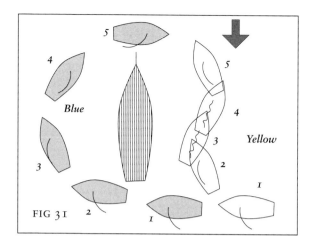

FIG 31

can do to prevent this manoeuvre in itself. She might not follow Blue, but attempt to luff and tack without rounding the vessel and then, if possible to tack again on to starboard to catch Blue as she clears the anchor line as shown in Fig 31.

As can be seen this requires considerable timing by Yellow; if Blue is at all alert, as soon as Yellow is committed to her manoeuvre (when she can no longer bear away for fear of hitting the moored vessel), Blue herself will bear away and gybe. She will then not only head off to safety but also be leeward, right of way yacht!

This type of manoeuvre by Blue highlights one of the principles of success, particularly in the pre-start: tempting your opponent into such a position that they are committed to a manoeuvre while you retain more than one option yourself.

There are two other opportunities for Blue. She can go initially to windward of the obstruction, or she can achieve a position where she approaches the obstruction close hauled.

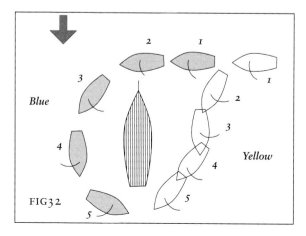

FIG32

In Fig 32, Blue chooses to pass to windward and gybe. Yellow will normally attempt to achieve position 5 which will force Blue to gybe, in order to keep clear. Yellow regains her control and continues to force Blue to the left. In doing so, Yellow faces a number of problems; primarily, she must achieve her intercepting starboard tack course far enough away from Blue so that she doesn't infringe rule 35. Notice that in Fig 32 Yellow does not alter course from position 4 to position 5. Her second problem is that, as in previous examples, she has to travel more slowly. Also, Yellow would rather not gybe, especially if the wind is anything but very light. This is because she will have to turn the yacht more, which itself makes the judgement more difficult. Going downwind slowly, without gybing, judging the new course and when to adopt it requires a great deal of skill, and probably depends upon Blue being very predictable.

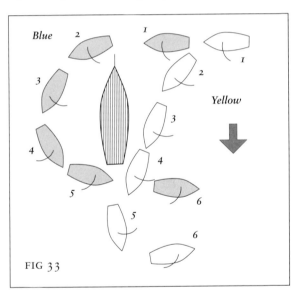

FIG 33

Fig 33 shows one possibility if Yellow doesn't manage to slow down enough. She will give the opportunity for Blue to luff between her and the obstruction and Blue's escape is complete. By the time Yellow gybes back into the leeward postion, position 6, there will be considerable distance between them. Should Yellow commit herself to one side of the obstruction too early, then Blue, instead of gybing to position 4, should luff and tack to achieve several boat lengths' clear water and ensure her return to safety.

In practice, whenever Yellow is close on the heels of Blue the most common choice for her is simply to follow Blue around the obstruction. At least that way she is guaranteed to be on her tail and 'in control', even if Blue escapes to the safety of the triangle.

At the beginning of this chapter we mentioned the importance of time awareness to the starting signal. One of the most common ways for Yellow to lose the start, even from this 'in control' position, is to become so preoccupied with the task of tailing that Blue leads her a merry dance until it is too late to return to the line to start on time. Blue couldn't care less how late she is to start, as long as Yellow is behind!

The final basic option for Blue is to approach the obstruction as in Fig 34, then to hail (and signal) 'Room to tack' using rule 43.

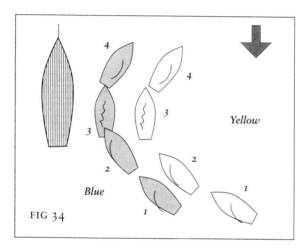

FIG 34

Before she is entitled to hail, Blue must ensure that she fulfils certain conditions contained within this rule. She must be close hauled and she must 'require' to make a 'substantial' alteration of course to clear the obstruction. She does not have to be on her close hauled course for very long though. We assume that the obstruction is solid enough that it would not be 'safe pilotage' for her to hit it! The larger the obstruction the easier this is for her to judge.

Yellow is best advised, as soon as she hears the hail, unless she is so close that her tack needs to be immediate, to respond 'You tack'. This allows her to sail on in order to tack into the best tactical position, and should Blue delay her tack she has infringed rule 43.2(b)(i), 'the hailing yacht shall tack immediately'.

Yellow must, of course, now keep clear until both tacks are complete and the obstruction is no longer an issue, and if there were any doubt, after protest any decision would go against her.

Just how difficult these manoeuvres are, and exactly how they work out, will always depend upon the type of yachts, the wind and current conditions as well as the skill of the crews. However, an understanding of the options available and some of the counter moves will enable you to sail with purpose in the pre-start, and that must increase your chances of 'winning the start'.

Reaching to the right

We start each of the next few scenarios again with Blue ahead of Yellow but this time reaching off to the right. This is much more common than to the left as the risk to Blue is much less, and is therefore the way that Blue will choose to go.

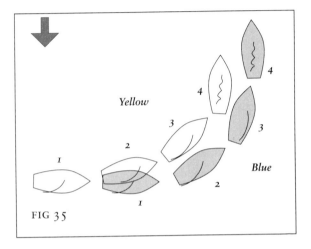

FIG 35

When Blue decides it is time to get back to the centre of the course, perhaps to start, her basic choices are to tack or to gybe. As Fig 35 shows, the initial problems of being able to tack are exactly the same as our previous scenario when the yachts were going to the right. Blue will be restrained to luffing only slowly, if Yellow has to respond, and she has to go through the period when she is give way yacht while actually tacking. Should Yellow give a little too much room then Blue may be able to establish herself on starboard tack. However, even if she is successful, Yellow will also tack and is likely

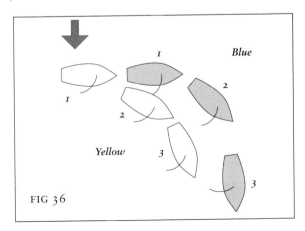

FIG 36

72

to be right of way to leeward, with the potential to trap Blue on the wrong side of the committee boat. For this reason Blue is most likely to gybe from port to starboard.

As Blue bears away, if Yellow is close enough she may still be able to prevent the gybe, initially at least. Indeed, in Fig 36, Blue would be forced to luff in order to fulfil her obligation as windward boat to keep clear. Again, if Yellow is too close she will have difficulty avoiding a large enough overlap thus giving Blue the opportunity to luff hard and tack.

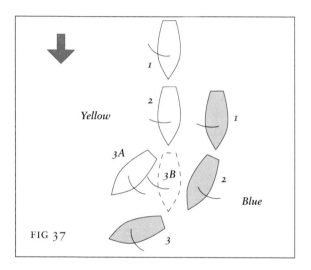

FIG 37

Fig 37 shows Blue, with more room than in Fig 36, having completed her gybe at position 2 and then Yellow choosing one of two options. Shown as 3A she has also gybed and luffs inside Blue. Because Yellow becomes give way yacht she will only choose this option if, either they are both late for the start or if her overlap prevents her from taking the 'dotted' route (3B), allowing Blue to pass ahead and hence Yellow retaining 'control'.

This scenario is worthy of very close examination which we will do with the help of Figs 38 and 39. Notice that the 'correct' position for the umpire boats has been included in Fig 38. The Fig also shows the clear water between Blue and Yellow as distance X and the lateral distance between them as Y.

It must be remembered that Yellow does not have to anticipate Blue's gybe into a right of way position. As soon as Blue completes her gybe, and there is a risk of collision, then Yellow must do whatever she can to keep clear. If Yellow holds her course until that point and then responds as best she can and succeeds in keeping clear, then Blue does not infringe rule 41, Tacking and Gybing. If Yellow is unable to keep

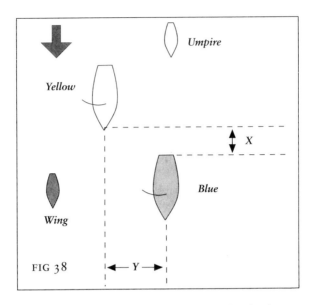

Yellow

Umpire

X

Blue

Wing

FIG 38

Y

clear, she will protest and Blue should be penalised. Skippers should learn what combinations of X and Y allow Blue to gybe in safety. Different yachts and different conditions will affect the numbers. With a small Y and a relatively large X, Blue will be able to gybe in safety, but will have no opportunity to force Yellow to gybe inside her.

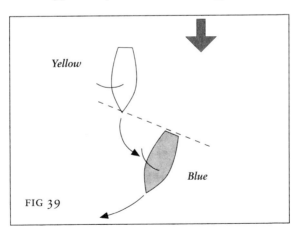

Yellow

Blue

FIG 39

With a large Y but relatively small X, Blue can gybe and have a much better chance of forcing Yellow to gybe inside. This will almost certainly require her to alter course (luff) after gybing so she has to remember that she must establish the collision course in time, so that she doesn't infringe rule 35.

In practice, if Yellow holds her course until Blue completes her gybe, the decision becomes quite easy for the umpires. Blue's umpire will call 'Gybe complete' which will be followed by Yellow's 'Responding'. If Yellow kept clear in a seamanlike manner, no infringement. If Yellow responded immediately and there was either contact or Yellow's response was unseamanlike then Blue infringed.

However as Blue bears away (as shown in Fig 39) she has to be very careful. In bearing away an overlap is created and Yellow will become right of way leeward yacht. If Yellow then luffs before Blue's boom crosses her centreline, Yellow can protest under rule 37, Same Tack, Basic Rules. The umpires will then be faced with deciding whether Blue was keeping clear. That decision almost certainly rests on what the umpires think is the distance between the boats the moment that Yellow commenced her luff. As the umpires are most frequently directly behind the yachts (see Fig 38) their judgement of the distance between the yachts will be significantly foreshortened and they are more likely to penalise Blue, sometimes absolutely correctly but sometimes there would be a different outcome if the umpires were able to view from directly above or even from the position of the wing boat.

While some decisions can be affected by this foreshortening we have also known a number of occasions when Blue has complained bitterly about being penalised ('I didn't gybe in her water') when the issue was decided long before she even started to gybe under a completely different rule.

To help with this problem it will be advantageous for the umpires to adopt the position shown as the 'pre-start alernative' in Fig 24c. They will have to be watchful, though, for a rapid luff from Blue after completing her gybe.

Whenever gybing in this situation, it is to Blue's great advantage to sheet in the main as much as possible. Not only does this reduce the loads on the boat because of the gybe but it ensures her gybe is completed at the earliest possible moment.

These scenarios illustrate some of the effects of umpiring. When umpires are judging the order in which things happen and how rapidly they happen, they can be very precise. When the umpires are required to judge distances, like all humans, they cannot be so precise. This is no different from the fact that the skipper of Blue, in Fig 39, will think that the yachts are farther apart than will the skipper of Yellow. All skippers should sail accordingly, it is part of the game of umpired match racing.

This is not to say that umpires shouldn't worry about this effect. All umpires (and crews in order to understand the problem facing the umpires) should take the time to go out on the water and find two yachts at anchor lying fairly close abeam. First approach them from abeam, position 1 in Fig 40, and judge the distance. Then go around and look at the gap from ahead or astern, position 2, and see what

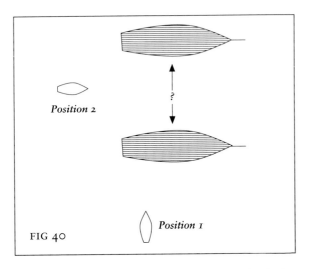

Position 2

?

Position 1

FIG 40

the difference is. When judging the distance instantly during a race it is even more difficult.

Rounding obstructions from a clear ahead situation is very easy for Blue. As when going to the left, obstructions create opportunities for the yacht ahead. But what happens when the yachts approach an obstruction overlapped? While we are out on the more common right hand side let's have a look at this.

Fig 41 shows Blue and Yellow overlapped, approaching an obstruction some three to four lengths away.

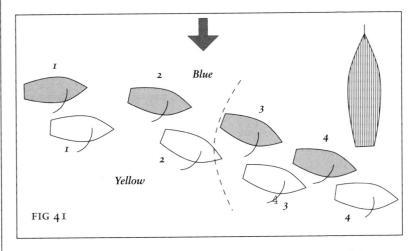

Blue

Yellow

FIG 41

At some point Yellow, as the right of way yacht, will have to decide what to do. In Fig 41, she chooses to pass to leeward of the obstruction. There will come a time when she is 'about to pass' the obstruction. Provided that Blue establishes her overlap before Yellow is inside two lengths from the obstruction, rule 42 will come into effect and Yellow must give Blue room to pass to leeward also. If Blue is at all close and Yellow luffs after she is 'about to round' requiring Blue to respond to keep clear, any decision should go against Yellow, even if she then gives enough room. The reason for this is that there must come a time when Blue can rely on Yellow not to luff or she could never risk taking the room to which she is entitled. When rule 42 starts to apply seemsto be the sensible time to restrict Yellow's right to luff although the rules are not specific about the point. Do remember though, 'about to round or pass' is not necessarily synonymous with two lengths.

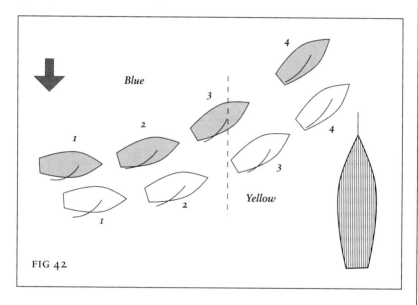

FIG 42

In Fig 42, Yellow has exercised her right to luff, slowly of course, in order to pass to windward. Blue must respond and as yet the obstruction is irrelevant. The only time that rule 42 will become relevant is if Blue achieves mast abeam and Yellow then has to luff above close hauled in order to pass the obstruction. Yellow can then rely on rule 42, assuming she had an overlap at two lengths, to override the obligation placed on her by rule 38.1, not to luff above close hauled, however, she must still luff slowly.

The final option open to Yellow is shown in Fig 43. She delays her luff to close hauled until she cannot clear the obstruction without a substantial alteration of course and may then call for room to tack. This is exactly the same as shown in the previous Fig 34. Remember that in this section we are not yet considering the approach to the starting line, so even if this obstruction were the committee boat, a starting mark, the same rules will apply.

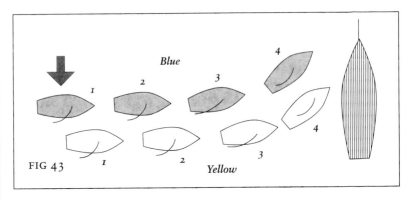

Blue

Yellow

FIG 43

It can be seen that obstructions create many issues, and later on we will examine some more options. With a significant number of spectator craft crews, skippers and umpires alike have to be at peak performance and, most importantly looking ahead to what is about to happen.

CIRCLING

Now that we have looked at the pre-start areas and the consequences of going to the left, (areas E and F, Fig 24) and to the right, it is time to take a closer look at that ritualistic dance of match racing: the pre-start circles.

As hinted at earlier (after Fig 24) the objective of circling (apart from using up time in relative safety) is to turn tighter than your opponent, to come out on her tail, 'in control'. But just how does this come about, and which way should the circles go?

Let's start by looking at two circles: one going clockwise, the other anticlockwise (Fig 44).

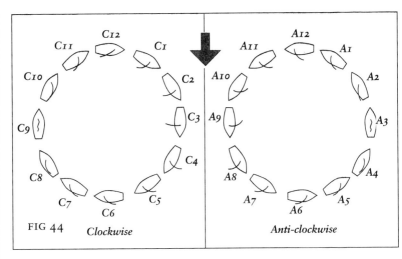

FIG 44   *Clockwise*   *Anti-clockwise*

The circles as drawn are not really as the circles would be on the water, but they will provide a reference diagram. Generally the circles on the water will be much tighter. If the yachts were circling clockwise with Yellow at position C12 when Blue is at position C6 it would not be uncommon for Blue to have to pull in her mainsheet in order to fulfil her obligation to keep clear as port tack yacht. The circles are in practice quite distorted and the circles of the two yachts do not necessarily lie directly on top of each other.

As anyone who has gybe-broached will know only too well, it is much easier to turn tight out of a gybe without losing boatspeed than it is out of a tack. Also, don't forget it is impossible to turn a yacht tightly without some boatspeed; the rudder doesn't work, and it is essential to use the sails to best effect.

It follows that one of your opportunities to force your opponent to break off the circles, with you 'in control' on her tail, is to luff fast enough out of your gybe to prevent her tacking. Yellow will achieve this if she can get to position C9 or A3 on her circle just before Blue gets to her C9 or A3, as shown in Fig 45.

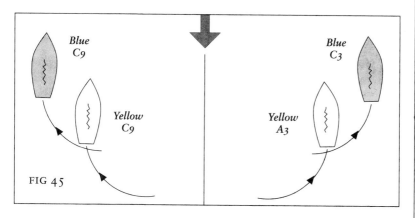

Blue
C9

Yellow
C9

Blue
C3

Yellow
A3

FIG 45

Yet again there are some ifs and buts. Unless Blue goes beyond head-to-wind, Yellow will establish a windward overlap and must as a consequence keep clear. Once Blue goes beyond head to wind she is tacking and hence give way yacht. Yellow is now obligated by rule 35 and any further alteration of course that removes Blue's only escape route (which may well be to continue with her tack) should result in a protest from Blue and penalty for Yellow. If Yellow overcooks her turn and goes beyond head-to-wind she will then be tacking and will remain so until she achieves a close hauled course, one way or the other.

Despite the difficulties, sometimes Yellow will succeed; when she does so and the circles are clockwise, Blue will be forced to remain on starboard tack and be driven off to the danger area to the left. If Blue is being caught while circling and she thinks this is a possibility, she would be advised to break off the circles at position C12 even if Yellow can easily follow her.

With the circles anticlockwise, Blue is far less concerned about being caught this way and forced to the safe right hand side, and indeed, as above, she has some chance of exacting an infringement from Yellow, so may almost invite Yellow to take the chance.

In the last two examples Yellow tries to use rule 41, Changing Tacks, to secure control. In the next two we see Yellow trying to use rule 36, Opposite Tacks. Fig 46 shows two typical examples: one in clockwise circles when the opportunity arises as the yachts are close hauled, and one while in anticlockwise circles as they are broad reaching.

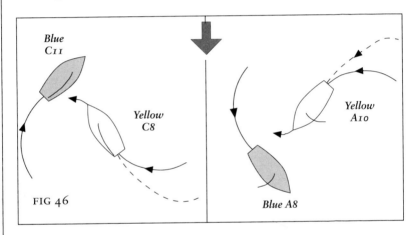

Blue
C11

Yellow
C8

Yellow
A10

FIG 46

Blue A8

In both cases Blue has just changed tacks, first by tacking and secondly by gybing. Inevitably the ability of Blue to respond is therefore reduced, which in one sense increases her vulnerability as the chances that Yellow can establish a collision course are increased. On the other hand, Blue is only required to respond as best she can and only once the collision course is established.

Assuming that Yellow establishes one of these positions, then alters course to avoid Blue and protests, how will the case be decided?

In practice there are two extremes. The first, the solid line track of Yellow in Fig 46, shows her continually altering course until the moment when avoiding action is required. Blue, without doubt, has not infringed. Secondly the dotted line track of Yellow shows her holding course for some time before taking the avoiding action. If that period of holding course is sufficiently long enough all umpires in the world would penalise Blue assuming she does not respond. As the period gets shorter and shorter so will more and more umpires 'dismiss' the protest.

In order to try to judge such cases with consistency, umpires' procedures should be as follows.

- Identify the moment that the collision course is established. 'Collision course?' ... 'Agreed'.

- The umpire identified with Yellow, the right of way yacht, must say when the course is being held, and continue to say 'holding course...holding course' almost continually while there is the issue.

- The umpire identified with Blue, the give way yacht, must say 'I'm doing nothing' or 'I'm responding but not using my sails' or 'I'm doing everything, helm up/down, sails backed/trimmed' or 'There's nothing I can do but keep going'.

The time taken to react to the situation and say these things should be the time it takes a skipper and his crew to react to the situation and hence can be used to decide the case. If Blue does everything possible after the collision course is set she has not infringed. If the collision course is set so close that her only option is to keep on going, she does not infringe. If she has an opportunity to respond and does not do so, then she infringes.

Yellow must be aware of this process and that no matter how consistent the umpires become there will still be the marginal case. Should she not finally avoid contact, she is at risk of infringing rule 35.

Both cases can vary, in the case of clockwise: Blue could be as far off the wind as beam reaching, while Yellow can be up to head-to-wind (although it is doubtful if she could retain sufficient momentum and hold her course long enough to win the decision while sailing much above close hauled). In the case of the anticlockwise circle both yachts can end up running by the lee and, providing neither gybe (allow the boom to cross the centreline, Fig 9) the situation will be decided as above.

This manoeuvre is normally carried out 'for the penalty' rather than for position. However the positional outcome is still worth consideration. In either case should Yellow force Blue to tack back on to starboard or gybe back on to starboard she will achieve 'control to the left'. Should Yellow misjudge, have to take avoiding action and not get the penalty, she is at risk from Blue tacking back or gybing back onto her tail. In practice the option from the clockwise circle is much more difficult for Blue to achieve, she will lose too much speed either double tacking or gybing from close hauled, and is therefore much safer for Yellow.

The final options to be considered while the yachts are circling is the use of rule 37, Same Tack. In order to use this rule Yellow must close right on to the tail of Blue and hence into the starting position of Figs 28 to 37 when those scenarios will come into effect and Yellow has succeeded in her objective of gaining control from the circle. When Blue realises this is inevitable (feeling brave) or possible (not so brave), she should at least ensure that she breaks away from either C12 or A6, to the right. By breaking early, before Yellow has got too close, she will at least have more breathing space in which to manoeuvre and get back to the starting line.

Before we leave circling there are some other considerations for both yachts. Don't forget how long to go to the start, how long it will take you to get there, and where you are in relation to the approach laylines. It is very easy to get wrapped up in the circles and forget the longer term, which at most is normally four minutes away. Someone on board should make a mental note of how long the circles are taking and calculate how many more you can afford to do without missing the start (and tell the skipper). Do you need to alter the boat set up on the approach? How long will that take? Maybe, in order to be at the correct point of the circle to break off for the start at the right time, preferably leaving your opponent too late or too early, you need to make the circles slower or faster. To achieve this can you alter boat speed or do you have to change the size of the circle? Trying to make the circle larger will give your opponent a greater chance to get inside so this option has to be chosen with care.

Despite all the options of circling, two things are certain: the helmsman and mainsheet trimmer should be different people, and practice reaps rewards.

Other same tack scenarios

In Fig 47, the rules allow Blue, the windward and therefore give way yacht, to swoop down across the bow of Yellow, as close as she dares, and then stop ahead of Yellow. Yellow must respond immediately and, as it would be easy for her to luff to keep clear,

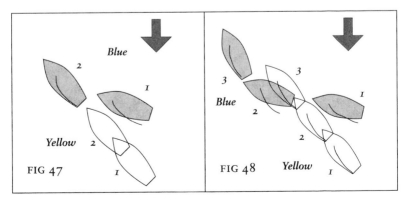

FIG 47

FIG 48

should she run into the transom of Blue, (the right of way yacht) Yellow will have infringed.

In Fig 48, Blue is even more aggressive as she clears ahead, continues to leeward for a few seconds, then luffs (slowly). While Yellow does not have to anticipate she had better be prepared to take immediate action.

The following scenarios are critical for match racing skippers. Seldom does a match take place without at least one of them happening. Furthermore, of all the penalties that are imposed, a significant number arise from these. You have been warned!

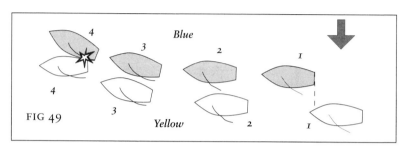

FIG 49

At position 1, Fig 49, Yellow gains an overlap to leeward of Blue. By position 2, Yellow has luffed slowly, giving plenty of opportunity for Blue to keep clear. At position 3, Blue is responding to Yellow's luff and might be able to keep clear by luffing farther, if Yellow luffs slowly. However, Yellow doesn't continue to luff: she bears away quickly, perhaps backing her foresail to help her spin, and her transom swings to windward, making contact with Blue.

This tactic, although causing controversy, was used successfully by *Kookaburra* (Yellow) against *Australia* in the America's Cup defence trials of 1987.

It has been argued that Yellow as right of way yacht infringes rule 35 by denying Blue her only avenue of escape, which she is not required to take until Yellow commences her bear away (ie establishes a collision course). However, the tactic of the quick bear away can be used to demonstrate that Blue has not, in fact, kept clear (ie she has left too little room for Yellow to manoeuvre). It is also a principle that a right of way yacht cannot infringe rule 35 when she turns away from her opponent.

Now let's look at Fig 50, in which three positions are shown separately for clarity. In fact, they happen within seconds of one another.

At position 1, Yellow is clear astern of Blue but travelling faster. At position 2 she establishes an overlap, much closer to leeward than in Fig 49. Immediately Blue puts her helm down, her stern swings and there is contact. Rule 37.3 states: 'A yacht that establishes an *overlap* from *clear astern* shall initially allow the *windward* yacht ample room and opportunity to keep clear.'

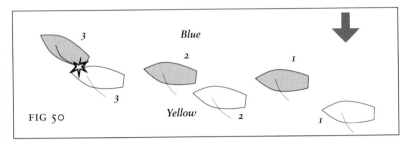

FIG 50

Provided that Blue responds as soon as the overlap is established she is under the protection of this rule. There has been much debate surrounding the question of whether Blue is allowed to overreact or not. At the world championships held in New Zealand (1990) the umpire team agreed that there was no limit on Blue's action. In other words, she was entitled to luff much harder than would have been required to keep clear, and if contact resulted then Yellow infringed. This has since been confirmed by the IYRU umpire calls' book.

Should the overlap be created by Blue bearing away at position 1 in Fig 49, then the obligation on Blue to keep clear becomes immediate as the overlap was not created by Yellow from astern. This prevents Blue from using what had become known as the 'fishtail' manoeuvre, whereby Blue would bear away to create the overlap and immediately use the new overlap condition to justify a hard luff swinging her stern into the windward side of Yellow.

The third case of this group is shown in Fig 51. From position 1 to position 2, Yellow and Blue are sailing close hauled, and there have

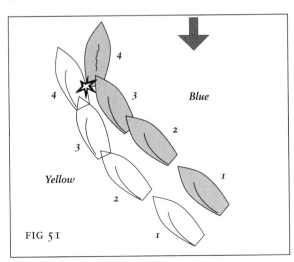

FIG 51

been no protests by position 2. The umpires will need to be satisfied that Blue is keeping clear. Perhaps the yachts are about 30 ft (10 m) LOA and there is 3 to 6 ft (1 to 2 m) between them in flat water and a light breeze. Now Yellow luffs slowly from position 2 to position 3. Blue immediately luffs, also slowly, the gap reduces and Blue continues her turn through head-to-wind. After she has passed beyond head-to-wind, but before her tack is complete, there is contact between the port transom corner of Blue and Yellow's starboard midships. Both yachts protest.

Rule 38.2, Luffing before Starting, requires Yellow to luff slowly, which she does, and 'initially in such a way as to give a *windward* yacht room and opportunity to keep clear'. Provided that:

1. Blue was keeping clear before the luff, and

2. she responds immediately to the luff, and

3. that had she not attempted to tack away there would be a reasonable chance that she would not have kept clear,

then Yellow is obliged to give Blue the room and opportunity to tack. Thus, in this case Yellow infringed and should be penalised. Umpires and crews are probably already aware that once two yachts get to within a certain, albeit close, distance from each other and they are making any way through the water then it is inevitable that contact will occur; even without a change of course or sail trim, such are the laws of hydrodynamics. If Blue fulfils the two conditions, 1 and 2 above, she should be given the benefit of the doubt with regard to 3.

Now look at Fig 52: Yellow luffs slowly, from position 1 to 3, Blue responds, and although the gap is reduced Blue does not tack away. The two hover abeam of each other for some time and then Blue decides to tack and her transom swings into Yellow. Both protest.

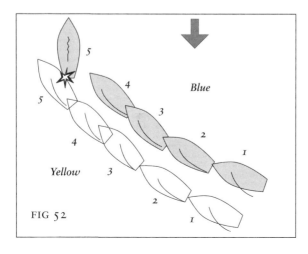

FIG 52

The umpires must judge whether during the luff Blue had the chance to keep clear: that is, was there a point when there was sufficient room for Blue to tack or was the closeness a result of her own inadequate response? The longer the period between Blue's luff and her tack the more likely the decision is to favour Yellow, and again the umpires should use the technique of talking to each other about the issue in order to decide. 'Do you think Blue did all that was required of her'... 'No, I think she let Yellow get too close, she could have done more'. All the time there is an issue the umpires must keep discussing it. 'I'm Blue, I am keeping clear, do you agree?' etc.

The last case in this group is shown in Fig 53. This time Yellow starts to bear away slowly. Blue luffs slowly, probably intending to tack, especially if Blue has been holding Yellow outside the left hand end of the line and the start is imminent. Yellow then bears away hard, even backing the genoa to make the hull spin and throw out her stern. The combination of both sterns swinging results in transom to transom contact. At the time of the contact Blue may, or may not be beyond head-to-wind. Both protest.

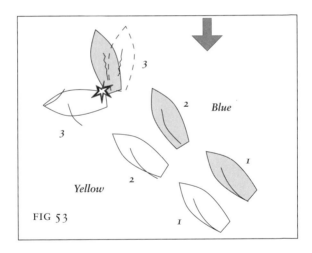

FIG 53

Here again, if the umpires are satisfied that Blue had allowed the gap to close further than she needed to, then she has failed in her obligation to keep clear, despite the bear away by Yellow. If Blue had done all she could since any previous luff by Yellow, including the tack when needed to keep clear, then Blue does not infringe.

We hope that it is now realised why this group of scenarios are so important and why they often result in penalties. It is worth noting that they are also the ones when it is most likely for both yachts to protest. They call for precise judgements from both skippers and umpires alike, and what is a very small change in the circumstances will result in different decisions.

The best advice to skippers must be; if you are to windward and the boats are close, do something immediately to increase the gap.

Sailing backwards

To be umpiring a match race between two Solings and suddenly see one of them 'go into reverse' and start sailing backwards, normally directly towards her opponent, can come as something of a nasty shock. (Not quite such a nasty shock as the other Soling gets, though, if she hasn't seen it happen before!)

If when umpiring, you are not prepared for such a thing to happen and yet protest flags are displayed, the decision tends to end up in the 'too difficult box', out comes the green flag, and then you go away and think about it for next time.

Why pick on Solings? Well, seeing one in action would make you believe that the designer had specifically set out to create a boat good at sailing backwards. Other yachts will also sail backwards but Solings are something special and now that match racing has been included in the Olympics this characteristic is being fully exploited by top skippers.

With a limited exception in IYRR Appendix 2, Sailboard Racing Rules, the rules do not mention sailing backwards. Some people have argued that while a yacht is sailing backwards her stern becomes her bow. If her stern becomes her bow, then her port side becomes her starboard side and hence she changes tack. What was luffing becomes bearing away, and vice versa. Few agree with this assessment, and therefore the yacht manoeuvring from position 1 to position 2 in Fig 54 is bearing away.

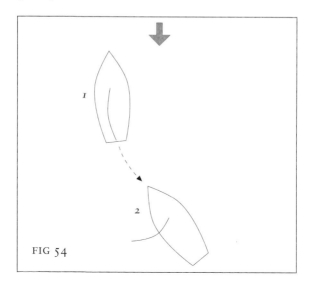

FIG 54

Other people will argue that when a yacht changes from forward to backward motion this is solely a change of velocity, not a change of course. However, for the sake of consistent interpretation the following important guidelines for judging situations (and hence also for a skipper manoeuvring against his opponent) have been agreed as follows:

■ Sailing backwards does not affect the tack that the yacht is on. This is solely determined by how she is carrying her mainsail, as discussed in chapter 2.

■ A yacht sailing backwards that manoeuvres such that her bow turns away from the wind is bearing away.

■ A yacht that goes from sailing forwards to sailing backwards, thus changes course and, if she is the right of way yacht is subject to rule 35.

These guidelines now arm us sufficiently to look at the basic scenarios of sailing backwards. However, before you try any with another yacht only a few metres away (or less), it is worth practising with each yacht in which you match race. Not all yachts behave the same. Just as not all yachts behave the same going forwards, with some having weather helm while others have lee helm, how a yacht behaves 'in reverse' depends entirely on the relationship between the centre of effort, the centre of resistance and how the sails are trimmed. We digress, though, this is not a sailing manual!

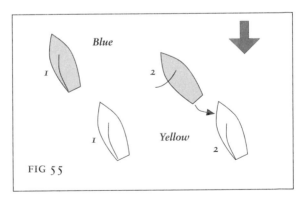

FIG 55

In Fig 55, Blue is clear ahead, forces her main out and reverses to the leeward side of Yellow. Yellow remains the give way yacht and is obliged to keep clear. Blue is required, by rule 35, to leave Yellow an avenue of escape. Yellow is required to take any avenue of escape left open to her. If Yellow responds immediately and yet does not keep clear, Blue infringes. If Yellow delays her response, or even responds inappropriately, and fails to keep clear, Yellow infringes.

It would be to Yellow's benefit in this situation, not to wait until Blue gets at all close, but to immediately try to copy Blue's manoeuvre. This has two advantages; if Yellow is able to copy Blue exactly then the relative positions between them will not change and, unless Blue can back up all the way to the safe triangle, Yellow will retain control. Secondly, by establishing stern way and by retaining as much distance between herself and Blue as possible she will keep her options open. With any speed at all, releasing the boom and reversing

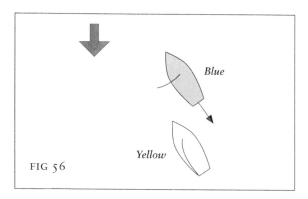

FIG 56

the rudder will cause the yacht to turn quite fast; if Blue gets too close Yellow's only option will be to luff and tack, with no boat speed and control will be lost.

Fig 56 shows Blue reversing to windward of Yellow in the hope of being able to escape control by tacking. This is a much less common occurrence because from Blue's point of view it carries greater risk. When the overlap is established Blue becomes immediately obligated to keep clear. Because Blue established the overlap by reversing from clear ahead she is not afforded the transitional protection of rule 37.3. Thus, Blue must leave plenty of room to allow for even a slow luff from Yellow. Soon after Blue has established the overlap Yellow will find it difficult to tack and effectively, if the yachts are out on the left hand side, will have lost some of her control. Yellow should attempt to match Blue and if possible close the gap to take advantage of her right of way, forcing Blue to escape forwards.

More on obstructions

As we have seen, the use of obstructions is a key factor in many pre-start periods. Unfortunately the yacht racing rules were not written with match race pre-start manoeuvring in mind. They were written solely to enable yachts, on the course, to be able to negotiate various obstructions in safety and without turning the results upside down. It was not envisaged that yachts would ever see an obstruction, sail straight for it and start circling round it in order to get away from a single competitor. The fleet would be long gone.

Tactically we have already covered what both yachts are trying to achieve: they are either trying to gain control, trying to maintain control or trying to escape control. This is in order to fulfil the two pre-start objectives. Obstructions provide opportunities, in combination with the special rules that apply at obstructions, to achieve these objectives and especially the need to escape control. It is important to understand just what opportunities are available and to what extent these are limited.

Fig 57 starts at position 1 with Yellow clear astern of Blue and this is the position as Blue comes within two of her lengths of the obstruction. At position 2 Blue gybes on to port and luffs sufficiently to clear the obstruction. Yellow on starboard is forced to alter course in order to keep clear of Blue.

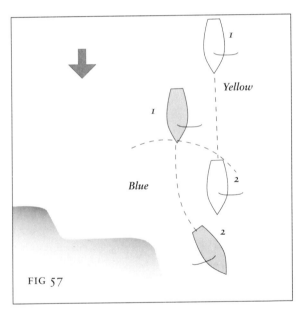

FIG 57

Rule 42.2, Obstructions when not Overlapped, applies and puts the obligation on Yellow to 'keep clear in anticipation of and during the rounding or passing manoeuvre, whether the yacht *clear ahead* remains on the same *tack* or *gybes*.' This clearly conflicts with the basic rules 36 and 41, and so it overrides them, Blue does not infringe. This situation is supported by IYRU case 68.

In Figs 58 and 59 we change the situation slightly.

In Fig 58, the obstruction has become a vessel, possibly at anchor (it makes no difference as far as the rules are concerned), which is surrounded by navigable water. The tracks of our two yachts remain exactly as in Fig 57 as does the application of the rules.

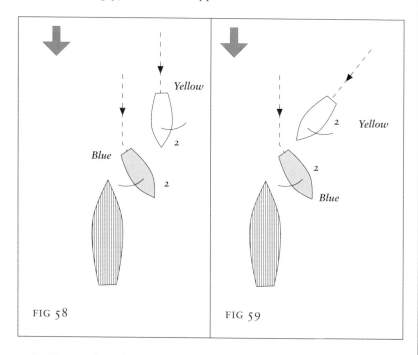

FIG 58

FIG 59

In Fig 59, though, it is clear that Yellow is setting a course to pass the obstruction on the other side. Rule 42 only applies when yachts are about to round on the same side. Blue must keep clear while gybing and while she is on port tack.

Going back for a moment to Fig 58, it is possible that Yellow could argue (given the chance in a protest room) that she, at position 2, was just about to luff to pass the vessel on 'the other side' and therefore Blue infringed. She will have no such opportunity with umpires who will undoubtedly judge the case on the track of the yachts some time back and that Yellow would be unlikely to want to give up control quite so easily!

Moving on to Fig 60 the obstruction is now right across the track of both boats. It might even be a lee shore with Yellow driving Blue away from the starting line. Again Yellow must keep clear and when she too has gybed she will be the give way yacht to windward and must now be wary of Blue luffing, slowly, up to close hauled.

In all these situations (Figs 57 to 60) it is reasonable for Yellow to have to anticipate Blue's gybe as she is obliged to by rule 42, for without the gybe Blue would foul the obstruction. It is also reasonable for the yacht astern to anticipate the gybe of a yacht around a mark of

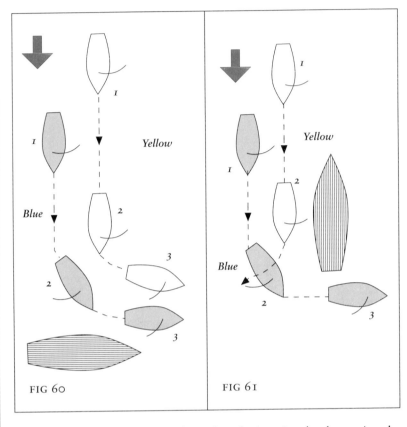

FIG 60   FIG 61

the course. In Fig 61, before Blue gybes she is quite clearly passing the obstruction without any risk and unless she gybes round close to the obstruction it will be judged that rule 42 has ceased to apply, and then she may only gybe if she keeps clear of Yellow.

If the intention of Blue is to gybe around the obstruction she will first of all need to remain close to it so that her intentions remain clear. She can also sail off by the lee for a short while or even slow down in order to force Yellow into an overlap on her starboard side. With careful planning and accurate execution Blue will almost cetainly be able to gybe around, but she cannot take liberties and hope for rule 42 to protect her.

In Fig 62, Blue and Yellow are approaching a lee shore, not exactly a typical fleet racing scenario. Blue is the right of way leeward yacht and may therefore luff to avoid the obstruction. If she chooses to gybe and then luff she must allow Yellow, overlapped, room to pass between her and the shore. If she leaves her decision so late that Yellow cannot safely follow, then Blue infringes.

In Fig 63 there are two moored vessels, C and D. They are anchored such that while there is a gap large enough for one yacht to

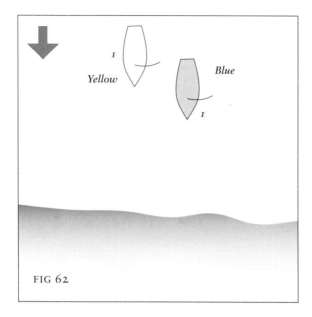

FIG 62

pass through, there is not enough room for two to pass abreast. Blue has established an overlap in time to require Yellow to give room for her to pass D.

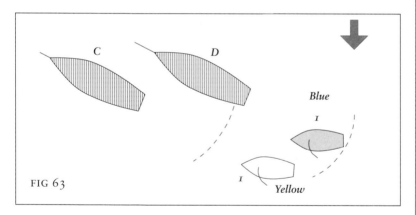

FIG 63

Is Yellow entitled to go through the gap? She could only do so by depriving Blue of the room she would require to pass D, so the answer must be no: Yellow would infringe by going through the gap.

Is Blue entitled to sail through the gap? If both yachts were to go through the gap then, in additon to Yellow giving room to Blue to pass D, Blue would be required to give Yellow room to pass C. However there will come a point in time when Yellow can no longer go through (without hitting C). If Blue now goes through, she is not denying room to Yellow and therefore does not infringe.

If Yellow bears away, at position 1, and succeeds in breaking the overlap by the time she comes within two lengths of C she will then be entitled to pass C close on her starboard side, including going through any gap that there might be, similar to the one between C and D.

As can be seen, it is possible to construct more and more complicated scenarios involving multiple obstructions, but we must stop somewhere. Certainly these situations happen very fast in all but the lightest wind, requiring maximum concentration and effort from crews and umpires alike.

Finally before we leave this section, remember that we have only considered scenarios up to when the yachts approach the line to start. Up to this point any committee boat that is also a starting mark has no special significance and can be used in the same way as any other obstruction.

The outer distance mark, normally at the port end, is most likely to be small. It is seldom large enough that the yachts racing would require to make a substantial alteration of course to avoid the mark when one boat length away. Such a mark, therefore, is not an 'obstruction' and thus rule 42 will not apply. While it is an infringement of rule 52.1(a)(i) to hit it (after your preparatory signal), you cannot claim room to pass it. Suppose, however you are already passing it to leeward and then you are luffed, such that if you responded you would hit it? Now you may hail 'Obstruction' (or similar) to curtail the luff as the mark does classify as 'any object' under rule 40.2, Safety Limitation.

5
Starting

This is the critical period when all the ground work has been done. Sometimes the match will be over bar the shouting but most likely the next few seconds are going to be critical. The time span of the period can be anything from a few seconds to a few minutes, depending upon the yachts, the conditions and what has happened during the pre-start. It is a period in which you must assess whether you can achieve the start you planned, or whether reappraisal is required. What is the best that can now be achieved? Maybe better than planned, maybe making the best of a bad lot. Whatever it is, you don't get a second chance at the start in match racing, there aren't any general recalls!

Luffing and sailing above close hauled

We have previously discussed luffing in a number of situations and in Chapter 1 we covered the ground rules of luffing before starting and clearing the starting line. Now it is time to put those rules into effect on the final approach to the line, which we assume to be to windward. The rule that determines the course that may be sailed and the luffing rights of a leeward or clear ahead yacht is rule 38.

In Fig 64, position 1, Yellow is clear astern of Blue. Blue is sailing and continues to sail a close hauled course, but is sailing slowly in order to time her start. Yellow is sailing above close hauled, but faster than Blue and establishes an overlap from astern. Clearly Blue is ahead of mast abeam and therefore there is no need for her to hail. Rule 38 only allows Yellow to sail above a close hauled course (while Blue remains ahead of mast abeam), if Blue does not have to alter course to keep clear. Keeping clear for Blue must be sufficient distance to allow for a future bear away by Yellow, together with the associated stern swing. Umpires should discuss this distance at the

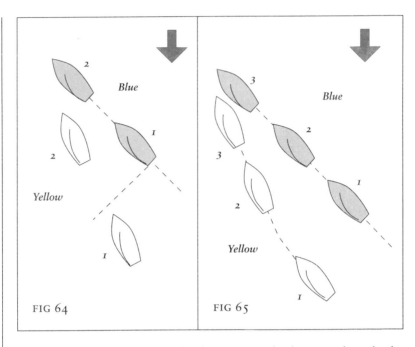

FIG 64   FIG 65

start of an event and agree 'the distance'. Only then can the rules be applied consistently. Wise skippers will enquire what this distance is.

Rule 38 is quite generous to Yellow, even when Blue is ahead of mast abeam. It allows her to sail above a close hauled course, and it also allows her to luff if Blue does not have to respond to her luff. This is the case in diagram 65. Yellow luffs from 1 to 2 but at such a distance from Blue that the luff does not cause Blue to respond. Yellow then holds her course, albeit above close hauled from 2 to 3. Should Blue eventually have to respond to keep clear, then Yellow infringes rule 38.1. Yellow must resume a close hauled course, or lower, before position 3 in Fig 65.

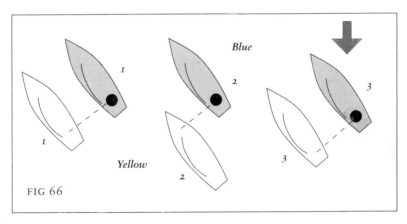

FIG 66

Fig 66 shows Yellow at position 1 with luffing rights. At position 2, Blue has clearly gained mast abeam position, Yellow may no longer sail above close hauled, if Blue has to alter course to keep clear. Yellow then gains some boatspeed to restore, at position 3, the situation to that of position 1, and she may luff again. This losing, gaining, losing, and regaining of luffing rights is a frequent occurrence when approaching the line. Blue is well advised to hail each and every time she establishes mast abeam.

Luffing at the start

As we have seen, rule 38, Luffing before Clearing the Starting Line, gives rise to situations where luffing rights can be lost and gained, during the existence of the same overlap, as Blue is first ahead of mast abeam and then behind. Rule 39, Luffing after Clearing the Starting Line, is different. Once Blue has achieved mast abeam during the overlap Yellow has to 'break' the overlap in some way in order to regain luffing rights. So when exactly does the changeover between the two rules occur and how does it affect the tactics of our two yachts?

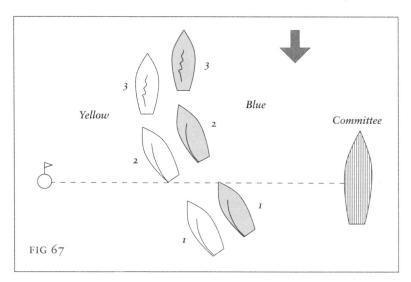

FIG 67

Fig 67 shows Blue and Yellow approach the starting line close hauled on starboard tack. The starting signal goes just before position 1. The definition of 'overlap' says that a new overlap begins when the leading yacht starts: position 1, exactly. However, rule 39 is not substituted for rule 38 until the leeward yacht or the yacht clear ahead has cleared the starting line: position 2, exactly. Provided that Blue has never been ahead of mast abeam during the existence of the overlap (from position 1 onwards), Yellow, at position 2, is freed from the shackles of luffing slowly and giving Blue the opportunity to respond. She may now luff 'as she pleases' all the way to head to wind.

It is essential that umpires position themselves to be able to judge mast abeam at all times but they must also judge when Blue starts and whether she is, without doubt, mast abeam at that moment. It may be critical later as the relative speeds of the yachts will often be changing rapidly until they are both up to full sailing speed. With the changes of speed may come changes in the mast abeam situation. Umpires, or better still the wing judges, should be in position to judge as Yellow clears the starting line just in case she immediately luffs violently.

To highlight this discrepancy between the commencement of the new overlap and the commencement of rule 39 applying, look at the scenario in Fig 68. This is not a common situation, but it has happened.

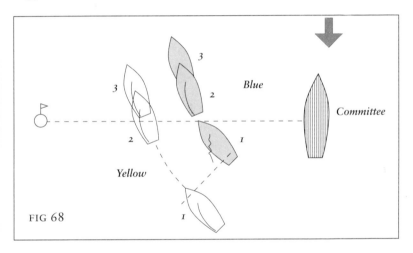

FIG 68

At position 1, Blue starts; however, she is close to being premature so she has eased her sheets and has no boat-speed. She is, without doubt, clearly ahead of mast abeam with respect to Yellow who is travelling at full, close hauled speed.

Yellow continues to sail her close hauled course and, without doubt, before position 2, Blue has fallen behind mast abeam. At position 2, Yellow, yet to clear the starting line, utilises her rights under rule 38.2 and luffs slowly; Blue responds and keeps clear.

Yellow holds her course from position 2 to position 3 but, as soon as Yellow clears the starting line, Blue protests and the umpires must decide if there has been an infringement.

At position 3, Yellow clears the starting line and now rule 39 applies. During the existence of the overlap, (ie from when Blue started), Blue had been, at one time, ahead of mast abeam. Despite

Yellow's right to be sailing above a close hauled course from position 2 to 3 (rule 38), she is not entitled to be sailing above a proper course immediately after position 3, even though Blue is now behind mast abeam and there has been no hail. Yellow therefore infringed rule 39.1 and should be penalised.

Starboard tack, starboard end

Fig 69 shows Yellow in a strong position if the starting signal is imminent, with Blue trapped to windward outside the triangle. Yellow will try to keep her there as long as possible. Blue really has three options. She can attempt to sail faster than Yellow, get clear ahead, and bear away for the line. This is the last option that Yellow should allow and must therefore adjust her speed to prevent Blue becoming far enough advanced to give her dirty air. Obviously the closer to the start line and starting signal they are the less chance Blue has of succeeding.

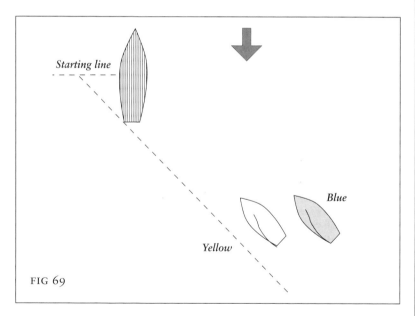

FIG 69

Blue can slow down and even sail backwards if necessary, establish clear astern, bear away and try for a leeward overlap herself, or settle for following Yellow over the starting line but close enough to be able to tack off immediately. Yellow will of course attempt to match Blue to keep her locked in to windward; but, if they are late for the start and should Blue succeed in getting clear astern, Yellow should accelerate and go for the line.

Blue's final option is to tack off, bear away and gybe back to the line, a disaster if they are late as it will guarantee Yellow a large starting advantage. If there is time, though, Blue should take this option early. Every second she delays will further strengthen Yellow's hand.

Starboard tack, port end

There are two different cases of trapping outside the left hand end while approaching on starboard tack. In the first (Fig 70) neither yacht is inside the triangle. In the second (Fig 71) the windward yacht is inside, and the leeward yacht outside, the layline to the pin end.

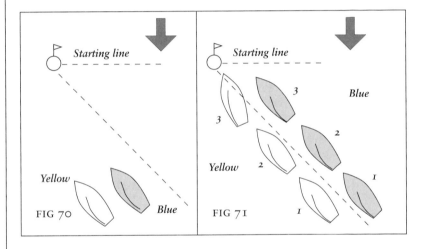

FIG 70

FIG 71

When both are outside the layline, Yellow will be using her luffing rights as much as possible in an attempt to force Blue to tack off early, leaving her the opportunity for a reasonable start. Similar to being pinned outside the right hand side, if there is more time to the start Yellow should bail out early, gybe round, and approach the line on port tack.

If trapped like this it is important not to turn a poor situation into a really bad one. Many times a yacht in a poor position does something unnecessarily in the hope of overturning the situation. The result, as often as not, is a three or four boatlength loss. In this case, don't bail out and gybe unless you have time to do so. Just hang in there and cross the starting line as close to Blue as you can.

In Fig 71, Blue is hoping for the 'big one', she makes the pin end of the line while Yellow doesn't. Yellow's main hope is that she can 'shoot' up to head-to-wind and clear the mark on the required port side. Note that Yellow is overlapped and Blue is not ahead of mast abeam at any time. Let us look at the applicable rules:

- Yellow is the leeward and hence right of way yacht (rule 37.1), and Blue is obliged to keep clear.

- The yachts have not started and so any luff by Yellow is governed by rule 38. Her luff must be slow and allow Blue opportunity to respond, but while Blue is not mast abeam it may be to head-to-wind.

- By position 2 they are about to pass or round a mark on the same required side but rule 42 does *not* apply when the mark is a starting mark surrounded by navigable water and the yachts are approaching the line to start, as in this case.

If Blue is ahead of mast abeam the end result is very different. Rule 38.1 now limits Yellow not to luff above a close hauled course. Even if the starting signal has gone, giving Yellow a proper course (which might justify her luff as when shooting a windward mark), rule 38 limits her to close hauled.

The outcome of all this is that, if Blue is ahead of mast abeam, Yellow may well not make the mark. If Blue is not mast abeam then Yellow is entitled to luff up to head-to-wind, slowly, and Blue must respond to keep clear.

Should Yellow initially have luffing rights and sail above close hauled she must be sure that Blue will not achieve mast abeam before she has cleared the mark. Yellow will then be compelled to bear away and hit the mark!

Port tack, port end

The situation in Fig 72 is very similar to that in Fig 69, when the yachts were approaching the starboard end on starboard tack. Again the leeward boat, the one nearer the safe triangle, is in almost total control. In both of these situations the hand of Yellow is significantly strengthened because, when approaching the starting line to start, she is not obliged to give Blue room to pass or round a starting mark that is surrounded by navigable water.

There is some restriction, though, on Yellow. While she is not obliged to give room, after the starting signal she is not permitted to deprive Blue of room by sailing above close hauled (or, should the first leg not be a beat, above the compass course to the next mark). In Fig 73, as soon as the starting signal is given, Yellow should not be above close hauled. In practice, so long as she immediately bears off to close hauled she is unlikely to be penalised.

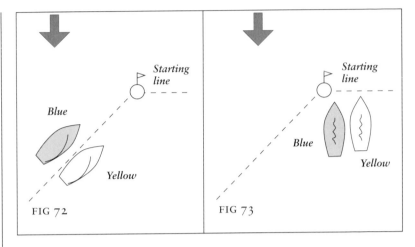

FIG 72   FIG 73

If both boats are a little farther to the right, such that Blue is not at risk of hitting the mark, then Yellow may hold her course, maybe in the hope of catching Blue out.

Port tack, starboard end

Blue and Yellow are approaching the line to start in Fig 74. Yellow cannot clear the committee boat, the starboard end starting mark, without a significant alteration of course. Ideally Yellow would like to call for room to tack. Unfortunately for Yellow rule 43.3(a) specifically forbids this call when the obstruction is also a starting mark surrounded by navigable water when the yachts are approaching the line to start and after starting.

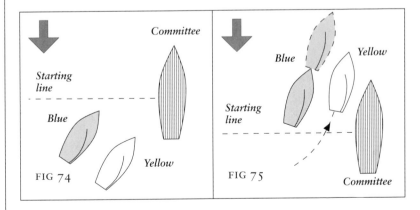

FIG 74   FIG 75

Although the anchor line is not part of the mark (by definition), rule 43.3(a) also forbids the call to clear the ground tackle of such a mark. You can hit it with your keel, rudder or whatever without infringing a rule, but you can't claim room to tack for it.

It is critical for Yellow to know if and when she can luff above close hauled.

Before Yellow has cleared the starting line rule 38 is applicable: if Blue is aft of mast abeam Yellow may luff slowly and sail above close hauled; if Blue is forward of mast abeam Yellow may not sail above close hauled should Blue need to respond to keep clear.

After the starting signal (Yellow now has a proper course) and after Yellow has cleared the starting line rule 39 is now applicable: irrespective of Blue being forward or aft of mast abeam, Yellow is now permitted to luff up to her proper course which will be as high as she needs to sail to clear the committee boat. If Blue is aft of mast abeam Yellow may luff as she pleases but if Blue is ahead of mast abeam Yellow must only luff allowing Blue an avenue of escape (rule 35).

Obviously it pays to have assessed the ground tackle prior to the start for the anchor line may not be below keel depth for many metres in front of the committee boat. Doing a depth survey for it immediately after starting carries a fair degree of risk!

Starting prematurely and returning to start correctly

In match racing, starting prematurely can be as disastrous as in fleet racing and can directly result in the loss of a match. However, as the object is to achieve a 'better' start than your opponent, it does not matter how bad your start is as long as his is worse. If you are premature but he is also premature and further from the starting line than you, fine. In this context, 'farther from the starting line' is only meaningful in terms of how long it will take to return and start correctly.

Let us look first at the race committee signalling of recalls as the sailing instructions normally amend the standard rules. In the event of an individual recall there will be a second sound signal but the visual signal will be specific to the yacht recalled and will normally be the same as the umpires would use to signal a penalty. If the yachts are identified by a coloured flag on the backstay, the race committee will use the coloured flag. If not, then placards with markings similar to those on the sails will be used. Whatever, they should be clearly visible from the far end of the starting line and mounted on sticks, not halyards, for instant display.

Depending upon your position, and that of your opponent there are really four possibilities for returning to the pre-start side of the line.

These are shown in Fig 76a to d. The outer distance mark is not shown, for the 'round the ends rule' will not apply and is therefore irrelevant. There is, of course, nothing to prevent a recalled yacht from going around the ends, but it's a long way round the committee boat.

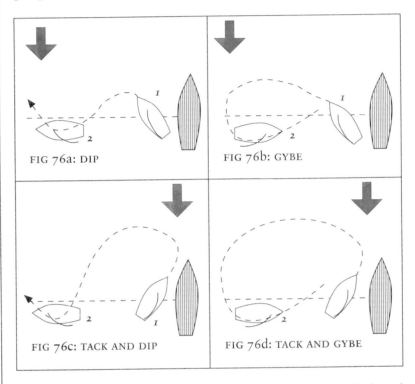

FIG 76a: DIP

FIG 76b: GYBE

FIG 76c: TACK AND DIP

FIG 76d: TACK AND GYBE

The four basic options are: 76a - Dip, 76b - Gybe, 76c -Tack and dip, 76d - Tack and gybe. Each one takes progressively longer than the previous one in normal conditions. However, if it is very windy, the distance lost to leeward in order to execute a gybe may be prohibitive. It is important to view the options not only for which is the quickest, but also which finishes with best boat speed and position. For instance, to execute option 76d, turning really tightly, only to be faced with having to tack immediately again to miss the committee boat and without any boatspeed, will surely maximise the price to be paid for a premature start.

Note that position 2 in each case shows the optimum position for 'clearing the line'. The idea is to lose the minimum possible to leeward, but the yacht will be turning fast at this point and should you fail to clear completely it will be very expensive. The safer option is to cross the starting line at an angle, concentrating on boatspeed, with a crew member watching the committee boat for the signal to drop, then luff to start.

If you select either 76b or 76d with a gybe and you are anywhere near the outer distance mark it is a good option to round the mark as you are then certain of clearing the line at the first attempt, without a major additional loss. If it looks to be possible that you will be recalled, think ahead, select an option, tell the crew and the loss will be minimised.

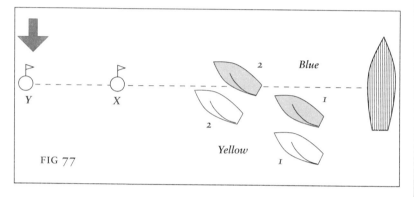

FIG 77

In Fig 77, Yellow has managed to force Blue over the starting line. Her gain will be determined by a number of things:

- Will Yellow also be premature and recalled? If so the yacht starting towards the biased end will make a great gain as while returning she can be making progress upwind while her opponent is forced to either follow or sail to the non favoured end.

- Will Blue have to tack to return or can she slow and dip return behind Yellow?

- If recalled, does Yellow have room to dip return (outer distance mark at position Y), or will she have to gybe return (outer distance mark at position X)?

- Will Blue have to round the committee boat?

There is not much point in Yellow forcing Blue over the line, being over herself and then taking longer to return than her opponent or being forced away from the favoured end of the starting line.

Starting with a penalty, or your opponent penalised

If you have been penalised during the pre-start period you are required to take your penalty (a gybe) 'as soon as possible after starting'. You do not wait until you have 'cleared' the line, nor does your penalty have to be completed on one side of the line or the other. The turn required to complete the penalty gybe may even circle one of the starting marks but if you have also been recalled then you must return to the pre-start side of the line, then start, and only then can you take your penalty.

In Fig 78, Blue has been penalised and Yellow manages to start to leeward of her, a good tactic.

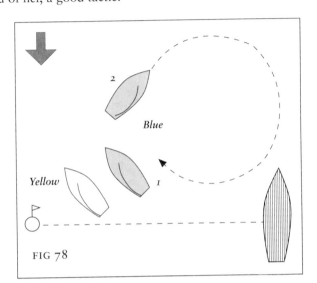

FIG 78

Blue is required to 'sail clear of the other yacht'. To do this she must either slow down to enable her to bear away astern of Yellow or she must tack. If she tacks as in Fig 78, she is now allowed to sail for a short distance to gain reasonable close hauled speed in order that the penalty does not become a full circle. She is also allowed to sail far enough to be sure that she is in no danger of fouling the committee boat or its ground tackle, but if the umpires decide she has delayed too long she will be further penalised by the umpires. Yellow may not protest.

After Blue has tacked to sail clear, Yellow is not prohibited from tacking, even if that would prevent Blue from taking her penalty, provided that she remains on a proper course.

While Blue is completing her penalty, Yellow is allowed to manoeuvre into a position that will give her maximum control when the penalty is completed, but if she deviates from a proper course and 'acts to interfere' with Blue while the penalty is being taken, she will infringe and Blue would be entitled to protest.

In Chapter 2 (page 19) we looked at the rules applicable to premature starters, and yachts returning to start. The situation is governed by rule 44, which can be summarised as follows: when it is obvious that a yacht is returning to start she is required to keep clear until she clears the starting line or its extensions.

Suppose that Blue is premature, while Yellow starts with a penalty to do:

- Yellow is obliged to take her penalty as soon as possible, but is allowed to ensure that she is clear of obstructions [Appendix B6, 5.3(a)].

- Blue will want to return to start as soon as she can, but when Yellow is sailing clear or doing her penalty Blue must not deviate from a proper course to act to interfere [Appendix B6, 1.4(b)].

- Yellow is required, while exonerating herself, to keep clear of the other yacht until she has completed her penalty and is on a proper course, in this case close hauled [Appendix B6, 5.5].

These two could well be in conflict and the rules make no provision for giving one priority. It would be most logical to apply the principle of 'first come, first served', which is applied between the yachts when both are taking a penalty.

When it is obvious that Blue is returning, Yellow should not initiate her penalty if there is a risk of collision; she is allowed to delay her penalty accordingly.

When it is obvious that Yellow has started to sail clear, Blue must not return to the line in such a way as to risk contact with Yellow.

6
On the beat

Immediately after the start there are two principal possibilities. Either one yacht will already be in control, or control has yet to be established. When control has yet to be established, the first objective is to fight for that control. Once control is established the object of the leader is to extend the lead to a 'safe' distance before the next downwind leg; the object of the trailing yacht is to escape control and to sieze any chance to gain the lead.

It must be recognised that there are times when it is appropriate to forget control and concentrate on winning the match! It is too easy, especially when new to match racing, to concentrate on the other yacht, being aggressive, and ignore all the other sailing skills. The times when an alternative strategy would be appropriate are when one side of the course is heavily favoured. Then you should fight for the favoured side rather than for control (they might be the same if your opponent has a similar view).

Establishing control is usually a matter of boatspeed, windshifts or use of current. This manifests itself as either a 'drag race' with the two yachts sailing on the same tack, or the yachts will split tacks searching for the favoured side. Obviously, if the yachts split there is little for the umpires to do except keep up with the race so as to be in position when they eventually come back together. If the 'drag race' is on, then the windward of the two yachts will be trying to sail over the top of the other, while the leeward yacht will be looking to backwind her opponent or better still to tack across, ahead. In the latter case the umpires should be constantly addressing the issue of what will happen when one tacks. If it is port to starboard, is there room to establish the new tack in time for the port tack yacht to respond? If starboard to port, will she clear? Constantly anticipating in this way will result in better decisions and fewer surprises. The issue will, of course, only be decided by what actually happens, not what the umpires *thought* would happen!

Once control has been established the yacht behind (say Blue) will be trying to break through to take the lead. When the separation is small, Yellow, who is ahead, might put a 'close cover' on Blue who may then be so effectively trapped that she can do nothing but sail on in the disadvantaged position. This will soon result in the loss of distance to the point where Blue is able to manoeuvre to break free, perhaps by tacking. Now Yellow has to decide how to react: should she tack to cover, or sail on for a while and then tack? The important point is that it is Blue, behind, that determines the actions of the yacht ahead. Yellow is invariably reacting to the manoeuvres of Blue, who is trying everything possible to force Yellow to make a mistake that enables Blue to take over the lead.

Close covering

One yacht is 'close covering' the other when not only does the yacht ahead maintain her position between her opponent and the mark, but she also forces her opponent to sail in dirty air and lose boatspeed. Fig 79 shows the effect that a close hauled yacht has on the air flow.

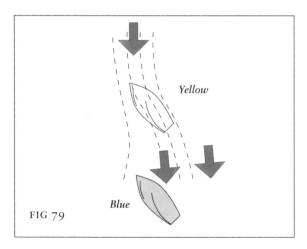

FIG 79

Two things are important: the direction of the flow and the velocity of the flow. It is this combination that determines the apparent wind that a yacht has to sail in. Without going into a detailed aerodynamic explanation, the farther apart the lines are the lower the air pressure and the higher the wind velocity.

To demonstrate the effect of air velocity on air pressure try this experiment. Take two pieces of writing paper and hold them one in each hand about 2 in (5 cm) apart in front of your mouth with the edges towards you. Blow down between them and you will find that they are forced *together*, not apart. The velocity of the air you have blown creates a low pressure in between the pieces of paper so that the air pressure on the outside, now greater than the inside, forces the papers together. It is for this reason that our two yachts were forced together when lying close alongside each other with some water flow between them; their keels are forced together.

The combined effect is that Blue, close behind, is forced to sail in backed wind that has also had some of its energy removed. The backing effect works just as well even if Blue is slightly to windward (safe lee-bow position for Yellow), although the wind in this position will not have lost so much energy and therefore the effect will not be so dramatic - that is, until the lack of pointing ability forces Blue to sag off into the 'wind shadow' of Yellow.

If we now look at Fig 80 we will see Yellow ahead of Blue, but by how much? If X is the distance that the bow of Yellow is ahead of the bow of Blue, and Y the distance that Yellow is to windward then Yellow's lead will be X + Y.

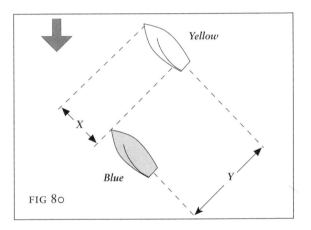

FIG 80

Blue will probably decide to tack off to clear her air, at least until the laylines are approached. Yellow now has to make a decision when to tack. By tacking immediately she will tend to be in the position shown in Fig 82, that is, with a relatively large X and relatively small Y.

Should Yellow delay her tack a little then the position will be more like Fig 81, small X, and large Y, but opposite tacks.

Blue's boatspeed and pointing ability will be much less affected in the postion in Fig 81 than in the position in Fig 82, hence her desire to tack will be less. If Blue is gaining through the tacks then Yellow must try to extend the sailing time between each without losing control – that is, to tack into a position nearer that in Fig 81 than that in Fig 82.

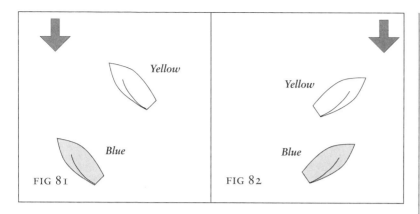

FIG 81

FIG 82

It is much safer for Yellow to tack into the position in Fig 81 when on starboard tack as illustrated. Should Blue make a gain as a result of the more distant cover, she will not be able to tack into the right of way (starboard) position. It is for this reason that, all other things being equal, the majority of match races end up on the port tack layline.

Loose covering and windshifts

The yacht ahead is loose covering when she manoeuvres to remain in control, between her opponent and the mark, but is not close enough to affect the boatspeed of the trailing yacht by her dirty wind.

Loose cover protects the yacht ahead, say Yellow, from two possibilities. First should Blue sail faster she will catch up Yellow, but only until the cover becomes 'close'. Then Blue will lose her boatspeed advantage as she becomes affected by Yellow's dirty air, and the gap will grow again.

The second (and most vital to understand) reason, is in order that Yellow can protect her lead, as best she can, in the event of a windshift. Hence this section is called 'Loose covering *and* windshifts'. All sailors, including the cruising helmsman trying to make a headland, well understand that windshifts are of vital importance. In fleet racing the windshifts give the race leader a real headache. It is not possible to cover all your opponents unless they all go the same way. The leader's decision must be based on a combination of: which way does he think will be favoured and which of his opponents are more important to cover.

Match racing may require many mental skills, but at least you don't have to work out which opponent to cover! It doesn't matter which side of the course you think is favoured, if you're in the lead - *cover.*

But how do you best cover? Does it make any difference if the wind heads or backs? Why does the yacht behind always seem to gain?

Understanding these points is a fundamental requirement for a good match race sailor. Often skippers have worried themselves into losing a match 'because they didn't have boatspeed', they then fiddle around with the boat and twitch until they *really* don't have boatspeed. It always seems to the leader that the trailing yacht is closing the gap, whichever way the wind shifted. As we will see, this could have been entirely the result of the covering position adopted and nothing to do with boatspeed.

Look at Fig 83, which shows the position (but not which tack) of Blue and Yellow beating towards the windward mark. Decide which is winning.

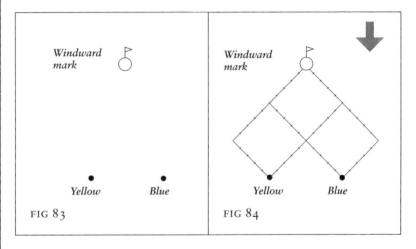

FIG 83   FIG 84

The answer is that it totally depends upon the direction of the wind.

Should the wind be as in Fig 84, the boats are equal. This is when the distance each will have to sail to get to the windward mark (or any other point at which the boats will cross) is the same. It is totally irrelevant on which tack each starts. However, as they are equal, if one tacked more than the other they would take longer to cover the same distance.

Of course there are some assumptions built into this figure. These are that the yachts are sailing at the same speed all the time and that there is no cross current.

Should the wind have shifted left (looking upwind) as in Fig 85 then Yellow is now in the lead. Regardless of whether she first sails to Y1 on starboard tack or to Y2 on port tack her distance to the mark will be the same. In both cases, this will be significantly less than Blue's distance. If the wind goes left, it favours the yacht on the left. The reverse would follow whenever the wind shifts right.

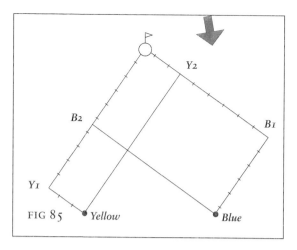

FIG 85

To emphasise this result and to show that the basic principle is independent of the starting point of the boats relative to the course centreline look now at Fig 86.

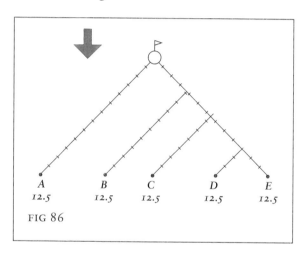

FIG 86

Here we have five starting positions: A, B, C, D and E. Underneath each is marked the number of units of distance each has to travel to reach the windward mark, in all cases this is 12.5. We have already shown this distance to be independent of the selected tack. Next look at Fig 87 where the wind has shifted left by 10 degrees.

Again we have marked underneath each the distance in our arbitrary units to the windward mark. We immediately see that E has to go farther than D who in turn has to go farther than C and likewise B. But what has happened to A? She was (refer to Fig 86) already on the port tack layline to the mark. She is unable to take advantage of the windshift and therefore has the same distance to travel as she had before. All she can do is to crack sheets and get there as fast as possible.

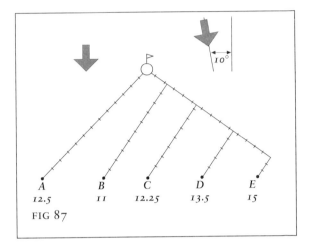

A
12.5

B
11

C
12.25

D
13.5

E
15

FIG 87

Of course, if the wind had shifted to the right then A would have lost out most, and similarly, E would not have gained.

The principle is confirmed then: if the wind goes left the yacht on the left gains, but provided she is not over the layline.

We have now seen which yacht will gain from a windshift, if they start from level, such as at the starting line. But just where should our leading yacht Yellow position herself best to protect her lead in the event of either a left or right shift?

It is important that we establish the answer to this in such a way as to understand fully the mechanism of a windshift. It would not be feasible to put all the possibilities into a book even three times the size of this one, but if we understand the problem then we can apply what we have learnt to any scenario on-the-water. We will need to go through a number of stages to achieve this. In all, we assume that the yachts remain within the laylines.

The next step is to find a method by which we can determine just how big the effect of a windshift is. Looking back at Figs 86 and 87 we can see that versus E, the others make different gains, B more than C more than D. The amount of gain gets greater the greater the distance between the boats. The distance between the boats is sometimes referred to as 'leverage', which increases as the distance gets greater. For our purposes we are going to use a distance of 10 boat lengths and we shall initially assume a tacking angle of 90 degrees. Later we shall look to see the effect of different tacking angles.

We start with the two yachts level, on opposite tacks. Yellow is to the left, in Fig 88, sailing on port tack with Blue to the right on starboard. With no shift they sail the same distance and meet at Y1, B1.

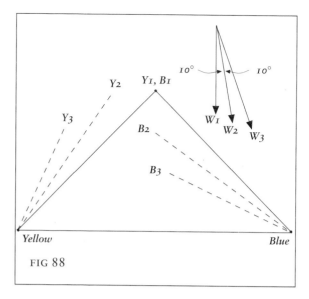

FIG 88

With a 10 degree left shift, Yellow is lifted and Blue headed and, as we saw before the boat on the left gains from a left hand shift, but look by how much! Yellow crosses the path of Blue at position Y2. As they sail at the same speed Blue will have travelled the same distance as Yellow to achieve position B2. Yellow has crossed 2.5 boat lengths ahead. With a 20 degree shift the gain is 4.8 boat lengths. These gains are made without any change of boatspeed or position: if the shift is instant the gain is instant. Incidentally even a 5 degree shift is worth 1.2 boat lengths.

We can put this another way for emphasis. If you sail away from your opponent on the opposite tack until he is just ten boat lengths away and then get on the wrong end of a 10 degree shift, you've lost 2.5 boat lengths.

If Yellow crosses ten lengths in front of Blue she has a choice as to how to cover, similar to when close covering (Figs 80, 81 and 82). Fig 89 shows the three options that we will develop further. The first option is for Yellow to tack immediately ahead of Blue so that they finish in positions B1 and Y1. Yellow can sail on a further five lengths to tack into position directly to windward of Blue at B2 and Y2. She can sail a further five lengths still, to end up abeam at B3 and Y3 (B3 is the same as Y1).

We realise that in all these scenarios the yacht tacking does so almost magically without loss of boatspeed. However the facts are that if Yellow, having completed her tack, is ten lengths ahead and then there is a windshift her position relative to Blue will be critical in determining the losses or gains she sustains, as we shall see in the following figures.

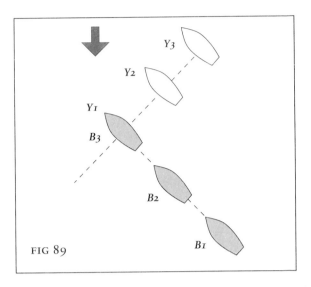

FIG 89

Fig 90 shows the case when Yellow tacks immediately ahead of Blue and then the wind lifts 10 degrees to the right. The dotted line shows the course of the two yachts before the shift and the distance separating them is X1, ten lengths (see Fig 80 for an explanation of X and Y).

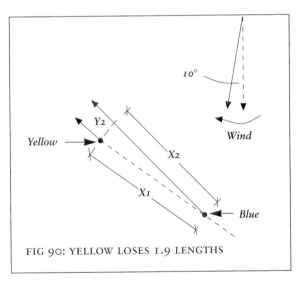

FIG 90: YELLOW LOSES 1.9 LENGTHS

The wind now shifts and the course of the two yachts is shown by the solid lines. Now Yellow is ahead of Blue, bow to bow, by a distance X2, but Blue's track is to windward of Yellow's by the distance Y2. Yellow is therefore ahead by the total of X2 minus Y2. This works out to be a distance of 8.1 boat lengths, a loss for Yellow of 1.9 lengths.

(For the mathematically minded who wish to check the figures or calculate their own for different distances and windshifts:

$Y_2 = X_1.\sin 10$ and $X_2 = X_1.\sin 80$; therefore $Y_2 = 1.736$ and $X_2 = 9.848$; therefore the lead equals $9.848 - 1.736 = 8.112$; but it's difficult to measure 0.012 of a boat length on the water!)

From the same starting point as Fig 90, the wind now heads (Fig 91). Again the tracks before and after the shift are shown dotted and solid as is the wind direction. Again it's a 10 degree shift but the change is different: Yellow gains 1.6 lengths, not quite as much as she lost in the lift.

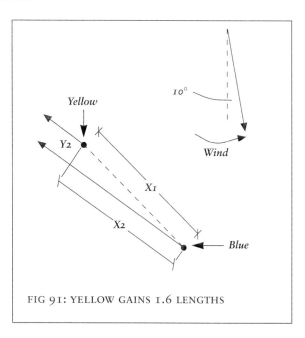

FIG 91: YELLOW GAINS 1.6 LENGTHS

Notice that Yellow is to the left of Blue in Figs 90 and 91. When the wind goes left, the left yacht is favoured. And when the wind goes right, the right yacht is favoured.

Should Yellow continue to tack dead upwind of Blue then we will have the situation of Figs 92 and 93. Now, whichever way the wind goes, Yellow loses 0.2 boat lengths. She loses both ways, but far less than in the lift of Fig 90.

It is worth while noting that in these two cases neither yacht is to the left, or right, of the other. The gains and losses are minimal and so represent least risk for Yellow who won't forget that although Blue may gain a little, she will end up in her wind shadow.

Now we move on to examine the third and final option.

This time Yellow has selected to sail on until she is abeam, as she may choose to do in order to minimise the number of tacks to the

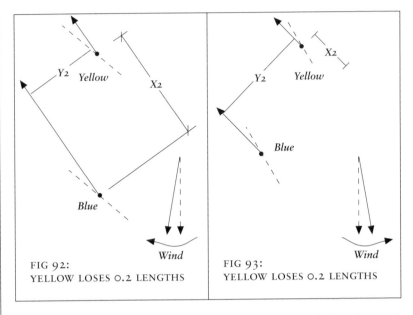

FIG 92:
YELLOW LOSES 0.2 LENGTHS

FIG 93:
YELLOW LOSES 0.2 LENGTHS

weather mark. She will be keeping her fingers crossed that the wind doesn't head, for fear that a 10 degree header will cost her 1.9 lengths (Fig 95), the same as a 10 degree lift when she tacked dead ahead earlier. Not surprising then that Yellow gains 1.6 lengths in the event of a lift (Fig 94). Yet again, with Yellow on the right, a right hand shift pays.

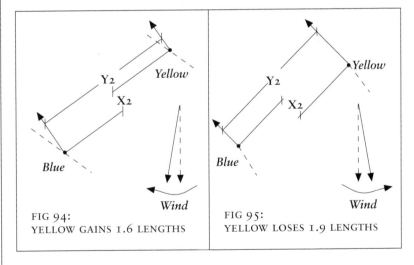

FIG 94:
YELLOW GAINS 1.6 LENGTHS

FIG 95:
YELLOW LOSES 1.9 LENGTHS

This may have all been rather confusing and, as we want to make some further tactical comments let's first list these results in a table. Remember that they are only valid for: a lead of ten lengths (but are proportional for any other lead), a tacking angle of 90 degrees (all the numbers get smaller if the tacking angle is smaller), and a windshift of 10 degrees (the bigger the shift, the bigger the gains and losses).

Cover Position	Lift	Header
Ahead	Yellow loses 1.9	Yellow gains 1.6
Windward	Yellow loses 0.2	Yellow loses 0.2
Abeam	Yellow gains 1.6	Yellow loses 1.9

There are first a number of general observations to be made about these results:

■ If after the shift the wind shifts back again all will be as it was. Although it may appear that Yellow generally loses this is only true if the gain is realised by Blue tacking.

■ If Blue does get her tacking right she should gain, up to the point where she collects some dirty air, that is. It is no use Yellow worrying about loss of boatspeed, she must expect to lose but retain control.

■ While we have only shown the figures for starboard tack they are of course exactly mirror image of those for port tack. The reason for using the terms 'lift' and 'header' in the table are that they then apply to either tack. Interestingly the phrase 'left shift is good on the left' holds good on both tacks, as does 'right shift is good on the right'.

■ If Yellow has covered abeam (or ahead) and both yachts tack simultaneously then her cover becomes ahead (or abeam). If she covered to windward and both tack simultaneously then the cover remains to windward.

It should be obvious from the table that if Yellow wishes to be conservative, then she should cover directly to windward. If she tacks either ahead or abeam, then Blue has her best chance to close the gap, and Yellow should always have some good reason for doing so.

Trapping and the use of laylines

In Fig 96, Blue is actually ahead of Yellow, being farther upwind, but is unable to tack; Yellow will round ahead provided that she clears the layline before tacking.

In this situation Yellow should take no chances at all. There is no need for her to judge the layline perfectly. She should keep going until she is sufficiently far over the layline to account for any possible headers after tacking. Blue, on the other hand, should already have anticipated this trapped situation and have been pointing as high as possible, and luffing if close enough to be effective without losing too much boatspeed, to force Yellow into tacking before the layline.

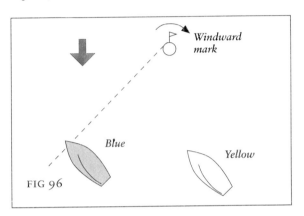

FIG 96

As match races tend to become shorter and shorter this problem for Blue is one that she must account for even before the start. A typical match race could be as short as 25 minutes and there are four legs with an upwind start and downwind finish, the first and last legs being slightly longer. Most of the yachts used for match racing are about 30 per cent faster downwind than upwind (speed made good) and therefore spend some 14 minutes going upwind and 11 minutes coming back down again. The first beat is the longer and could take up to 8 minutes. If the course is square to the wind, it takes only 4 minutes to get to the first layline.

If you decide to start to leeward of your opponent, even in the safe lee-bow position you either have to force her to tack off, or gain sufficient distance to be able to tack across before you get to the position in which Blue finds herself in Fig 96. This problem will be made much worse if there is any current with the beat. Not only will the layline arrive sooner but Yellow will be able to pinch and hang in there much longer.

Knowing just how long you have to sail to reach the layline is often a vital piece of information which will dictate the tactics.

The slam dunk

What a wonderful phrase! Before we move on to tacking duels it is important to understand the rules that apply to the 'slam dunk'. A tack is a true slam dunk when it is executed in such a way that the other yacht can neither tack away nor break through to leeward; she is then forced to 'take dirt'.

First we shall look at a starboard tack yacht (Blue), crossing ahead of a dipping port tack yacht (Yellow) and immediately tacking. Fig 97 shows this starting position. Faced with this situation, Yellow would be wise to bear away early in order that she can be luffing as Blue crosses her bow.

By position 2, shown in Fig 98, Blue has luffed to head-to-wind but remains on starboard tack. Her luff and any stern swing may require Yellow to bear away further.

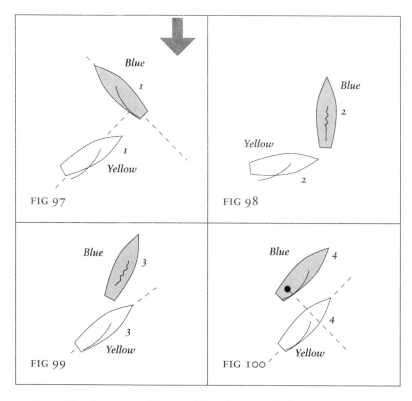

FIG 97

FIG 98

FIG 99

FIG 100

Once Blue has passed beyond head-to-wind she becomes the give way boat, tacking. Yellow will want to luff up as far as possible, but now she is constrained by rule 35. Clearly if she were to luff fast head-to-wind in Fig 99 then there would be no avenue of escape for Blue, and therefore Yellow would infringe. However Blue really must respond as best she can. Sometimes that may require her to luff back towards head to wind before reaching her close hauled course. Sometimes her only avenue of escape will be to stop bearing away and sometimes she will have no option but to continue her tack. Sometimes it may be unseamanlike for her to 'go back'.

There is no doubt that all these 'sometimes' make life difficult for skippers and umpires alike. For this reason there is much sense in giving the benefit of any doubt as follows. Up to the time when Blue is beyond head-to-wind Yellow is required to keep clear. As we have discussed previously this means more than avoiding contact and any doubt should go against her unless she is observed to be bearing away. Once Blue is beyond head to wind she is required to keep clear and there is an onus clause in the rules that she must satisfy. Cases of doubt will go against Blue.

All this requires some smart umpiring - Solings go from close hauled to closed hauled on the new tack in less than 3 seconds quite frequently, and even the yachts used on the grand prix circuit can take less than 5 seconds.

Once we get to the situation in Fig 100, when Blue has completed her tack and is now windward boat, the situation becomes clearer. Yellow will be travelling faster, and the situation will be changing quickly but it is vital for all to know if, at the exact moment of completion of the tack, Blue is ahead of mast abeam or, if there is any doubt, whether she has signalled. If there is a wing boat, either they or the umpire boat should be in the exact position to make the judgement. If the umpire boat is operating on its own, the umpires will have to judge from a less than ideal position. As Blue completes her tack, Yellow may always luff up to close hauled. If Yellow has luffing rights and she has managed to be close up to Blue then she should luff further without delay, before Blue has a chance to build up boatspeed and respond. It is this risk combined with the problems of Fig 99 that ensure that Blue is a little conservative with her 'slam dunk'.

As can be seen, the manoeuvre requires great skill and, like all skills requires practice. It is such practice that often results in damage on the practice days before major regattas for the crews are getting used to the handling characteristics of the boats to be used.

Should Yellow attempt to tack on to port from position 3, then she must keep clear while doing so.

The lee-bow tack

Fig 101 shows a lee-bow tack, so called because Yellow, the tacking yacht, is able to establish the safe lee-bow position, which will, sooner or later, force Blue to tack off. Just how close can Yellow tack without infringing?

This is how the two umpires will call: Yellow's umpire will say 'luffing...head-to-wind...tack complete', while Blue's umpire, while concentrating on the helm of his yacht, will say, 'Holding course...holding course...luffing'. These calls correspond with positions 1, 2 and 3 in Fig 101.

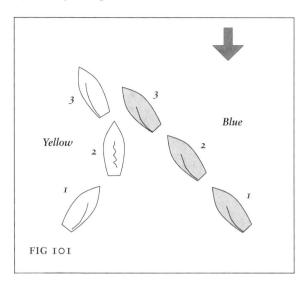

FIG 101

If the call 'Complete' from Yellow comes before 'Luffing' from Blue, then the tack was certainly OK. If the calls come the other way round, then the umpires have to assess if the helmsman of Blue made a reasonable decision to avoid contact. This they can only judge by being in a position to monitor the gap at the time of the luff. If Blue luffs unnecessarily early, while the gap is large, the umpires will be unable to judge and would not penalise Yellow. If however they are in doubt then the decision should be 'no penalty'. The match racing appendix no longer requires the umpires to apply the principle of the onus clause of rule 41.3. Thus when in doubt the umpires should follow the usual principle of not penalising.

Blue is well advised to luff and protest rather than risk collision. By taking this action there is no way that she can be penalised - always a good position to be in.

If we look at Fig 102 we will see a manoeuvre by Blue which can often eliminate the threat of the lee-bow tack. As Blue at position 1 sees Yellow luff to tack, she bears away. This has three effects: Yellow is forced to respond as give way yacht by tacking faster and tighter than she would have done normally, thus losing more boatspeed; Blue will gain a little speed; and Blue gives herself room to luff after Yellow has completed her tack without losing speed. The sum of these effects can be that Blue ends up in a controlling windward position. While of great tactical advantage, Blue is far less likely to 'get a decision' against Yellow but this is frequently the best option.

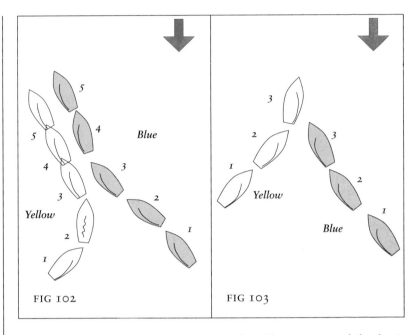

FIG 102   FIG 103

Fig 103 shows another manoeuvre that Blue can use while she is right of way starboard tack yacht. At position 1 and 2, Yellow on port tack is going to cross clear ahead, just, but sufficient to fulfil her obligation to keep clear. Blue now luffs, which forces a response from Yellow. Provided that Yellow's response is not unseamanlike, then Blue does not infringe rule 35. Blue can luff up to head to wind and Yellow must still respond and tack if necessary to keep clear. Once Yellow has passed through head-to-wind, Blue may also continue to turn and tack without infringing. It is a useful manoeuvre for Blue if she wishes to stay on the right hand side of the course and obviously the next crossing of the two will find her on starboard tack again.

Tacking duels

When you are the yacht behind and being covered, the longer you remain there the happier your opponent will be. You should tack, even though your opponent will tack to cover. You should tack again, and again and again.

As the yacht behind there are three ways in which you can gain: first, you can just tack the boat better than your opponent; secondly, you can gain by choosing the time of your tacks to take advantage of windshifts and waves; thirdly you can hope for a mistake from your opponent.

Apart from simply attempting to gain distance, the yacht behind should also be trying to get her tacks out of phase with her opponent. She may then sail largely unaffected by dirty wind although in order to remain out of phase she will have to then tack in time with her opponent.

Throughout a duel, the distance should be monitored. While you are gaining or getting out of phase, keep the duel going. If you are losing, try to stop the duel when you are least affected by the wind shadow and going the way most likely to give you a beneficial lift.

If you are the leading yacht in a duel, you need to know which way you want to force your opponent to go. As previously, this will be to the left unless there is a good reason otherwise. You encourage your opponent to go one way by covering abeam rather than to windward on that tack. If you cover abeam on starboard tack and then the wind shifts left, so you are headed; you will lose, as shown in the section on windshifts.

If you are behind, it is much easier to break through if you can get the tacks out of phase. It may be worth while sacrificing a little distance in order to achieve this by two tacks very close together, or the other classic match race manoeuvre: the dummy tack.

A dummy tack is accomplished by luffing as if to tack, but then falling back onto the original tack. When going into a dummy be sure that the crew know and are prepared for it - dummies can backfire! There is little doubt that the time a dummy tack is most likely to be effective is very early in the duel. By definition it requires a degree of unawareness from the yacht in front. You need to watch the skipper or tactician; are they watching you the whole time, or do they look away once the tack is initiated?

Sometimes one will luff, and so will the other. Halfway up the beat they will be sitting there almost head-to-wind going nowhere. The yacht astern hopes that the leader will fall off, either to port or starboard, first and still with enough control of the yacht to chose the other. The best way to make this work is to luff just after your opponent has hit a wave and has lost boatspeed.

As for the umpires, during a tacking duel the time will pass quite quickly, as there is plenty to do. Each time a yacht tacks call: 'Luffing...head-to-wind...tack complete....give way port [or right of way starboard].' If the tacks are very fast a slight shorthand can be agreed between the umpires: 'Luffing, head-to-wind, port (starboard).' Just saying 'Port' or 'Starboard' is the signal that the tack is complete and indicates which tack the yacht is on.

It is especially important to register exactly when the tack to starboard is completed if this will require an immediate response from the other on port. What might that response be? There are three options: tack, bear away, or keep going. It is important to remember that to keep going may be the only avenue the newly obligated yacht has, in which case, she must be allowed to do so. It is most difficult to judge as it requires the umpires to assess what would have happened if the yacht had borne away or attempted to tack. It is never easy to judge what the result would have been had the yachts behaved differently. In a case like this the port tack yacht must be given the benefit of any doubt.

Eventually the two yachts will approach the windward mark and that is where Chapter 7 begins.

7
The windward mark

For many years, most yacht races have required yachts to round marks to port, especially windward ones. The reason for this is the problems faced by a yacht trying to round the mark while on port tack. In large fleets this can be nothing short of dangerous, and thus in most fleet races marks are set to port. In match racing, however, starboard roundings can add interest in that they give a slight advantage to the yacht behind and, as a consequence have now become the standard. Therefore we give the associated scenarios priority. We will not, however, completely ignore port roundings.

Approaching the windward mark

During the later stages of the beat (which as we have seen may not be very long after the start) the approach to the windward mark must be considered.

If the mark is to be rounded to starboard, then you will be on port tack as you round. If you are on port tack now, you must have an even number of tacks to do before you round; but if you are on starboard you must have an odd number of tacks to do. It is desirable to have sufficient time on the last tack into the mark to prepare for the spinnaker hoist and to be at full speed before having to bear away.

In Fig 104, Blue is just crossing ahead of Yellow. If Blue decides to tack to cover to windward she will have to complete three tacks into the mark. Yellow will only have to complete two. Blue, as the leading yacht not affected by wind shadow, always has the choice of continuing to the layline and reducing her number of tacks to one. Yellow cannot prevent this, but she can ensure that Blue cannot take this option and cover to windward at the same time.

In Fig 105, Blue has again crossed just ahead and this time has potentially fewer tacks to the mark, unless Yellow takes the risk of going to the layline.

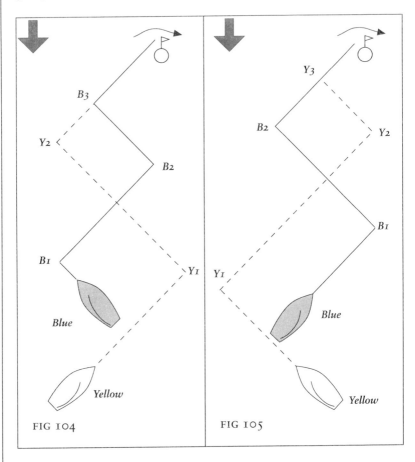

FIG 104   FIG 105

Figs 106 and 107 are different as both yachts are on the same tack and therefore have the same number of potential tacks to the mark.

In Fig 106 with both yachts on port tack, Yellow should sail at least as far as the dotted track. This will ensure that if Blue chooses to cover all the way, her final approach will be on starboard and hence a slow rounding. Yellow might even succeed in coaxing Blue over her layline for an even bigger gain. Blue, of course, can choose to tack earlier, but only at the expense of direct windward cover and therefore not without some risk.

In Fig 107 Yellow must be most careful not to tack such that Blue can both lay the mark perfectly and maintain windward cover. This would probably cost Yellow the match. If Yellow cannot tack early enough to give Blue the choice either to cover or go for the layline then she should go for the layline herself. Fig 107 is perfect for Blue and therefore bad news for Yellow, who should keep going hoping that Blue will either tack before the layline or will sail well beyond the layline. She must force Blue to make this judgement in the hope of error.

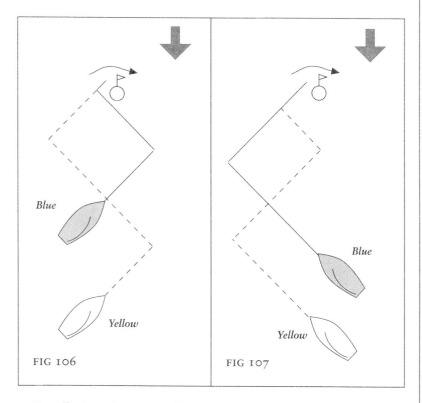

FIG 106   FIG 107

Equally it is disastrous for Yellow if she tacks just short of the layline and has to do two tacks - or even to shoot the mark. She must judge her own tack to take account of dirty air from Blue, and so needs to overstand a little.

Unless Blue makes a big mistake Yellow is unlikely to take the lead by the windward mark. She must concentrate on being in a good position to attack on the next downwind leg.

Somewhere towards the end of the beat it is necessary to assess the run. We will look at the tactics on the run later but it is essential to know if you want to set off down the run on port tack or starboard tack in order to set the boat up for a bear away set or gybe set (or even a tack/gybe set if you find yourself on the starboard layline!).

All of these approaches will be exactly mirrored for port-hand roundings.

Rounding the windward mark - port or starboard

As we look at the actual rounding, the rules become more important than the tactics. The object of each is to round the mark without infringing. Again we look at the starboard rounding but will make comments relevant to port-hand marks as we go along.

Figs 108 to 110 show three different scenarios, but they are actually a progression, each requiring a greater rules knowledge than the one before.

First, Fig 108, Blue and Yellow are approaching the windward mark both on port tack. They are overlapped, but Blue is behind mast abeam at all times. Yellow therefore has full luffing rights and may exercise these at any time. In this case she chooses to do so in order to shoot the mark in the last few seconds; Blue must respond and keep clear. Yellow may be well advised to luff earlier. If she needs two luffs she may still make the mark and if she only needs the one then by luffing earlier she will round the mark with less turn required to the next course. The rules permit her to luff at any time.

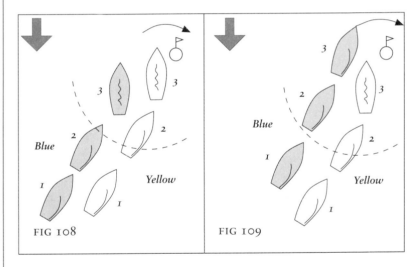

FIG 108

FIG 109

In Fig 109, Blue is ahead of mast abeam and we shall assume that she has signalled. Yellow is obliged not to sail above her proper course but her luff, at position 2 to 3, is the course she would sail, in the absence of Blue, and *is* therefore her proper course. Yellow is also subject to rule 35 while Blue is ahead of mast abeam and cannot 'luff as she pleases' unless Blue is able to respond. While Yellow might be able to argue that, even in the absence of Blue she would have luffed earlier to make the mark, the farther she is from the mark when she luffs the less likely that her course will be viewed as a proper course. Therefore she is at greater risk of penalty should Blue protest.

In both these cases Yellow also has the right to room as provided in rule 42 but as this is not in conflict with the basic rule it is irrelevant. These two can be exactly mirrored onto a port hand rounding with the approach on starboard tack.

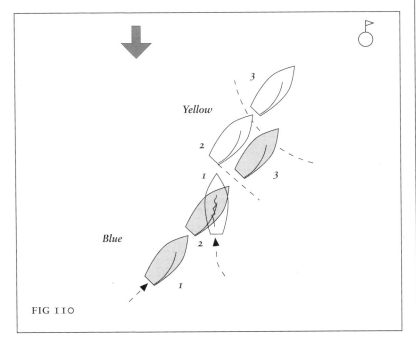

FIG 110

In Fig 110, Blue is on her familiar port tack approach. Yellow cannot force Blue to tack, nor can she risk tacking to leeward. She crosses ahead of Blue and then tacks. Her tack is completed at position 2, when she is clear ahead and just entering the two length circle. Blue is travelling faster and cannot avoid a late overlap by luffing. This set of circumstances fulfils the requirement for rule 42.3(a)(ii) to apply, and Yellow is obliged to give room to Blue. The case can be mirrored exactly for port roundings.

Should Blue and Yellow be on the same tack approaching the mark and Blue clear astern as Yellow enters the two length circle, Blue is obliged to keep clear - even if she later obtains an overlap. Now there is conflict between rule 42 and the basic rules, and rule 42 overrides.

Starboard rounding

So much for the scenarios that work out pretty much the same whichever side the windward mark is to be passed. We now move on to the case that causes difficulties with starboard roundings and is shown as four steps in Figs 111 to 114.

In Fig 111, Yellow is approaching the mark close hauled on starboard tack, and Blue on port tack. In this position, Blue is crossing clear ahead of Yellow. Should there be an incident at this stage, Blue infringes rule 36. (Note that rule 42 does not apply at all to yachts on opposite tacks on a beat.)

In Fig 112, Yellow has luffed, between Blue and the mark, but has not yet passed beyond head-to-wind and is therefore on starboard tack. At first sight it may appear that Yellow is at risk of infringing rule 35, but if her luff is 'rounding a mark' then rule 35 does not apply. If there is an incident at this point the umpires must address the luff of Yellow. If it were part of mark rounding then Blue infringes rule 36; if it were not part of the rounding Yellow infringes rule 35 (assuming Blue has no opportunity to respond).

In Fig 113, Yellow goes beyond head-to-wind and becomes the give way yacht, required to keep clear. Furthermore, Blue - who is rounding the mark - is not restricted by rule 35 and may therefore bear away. Now, if there is an incident here, which infringed? This is far from easy to decide. On the face of it, Yellow infringed as tacking yacht, rule 41. However, if she were given the opportunity to tell her story in a protest hearing she may well argue as follows. By the time she had reached position 3 in Fig 112, a collision was inevitable unless she continued to turn to starboard and her tack therefore was to avoid contact. She was therefore compelled wrongfully to infringe rule 41 and should be exonerated and Blue penalised.

In Fig 114, things have become a little easier again. Yellow has completed her tack and is now right of way leeward, but must continue to bear away to a proper course around the mark if Blue is ahead of mast abeam, as is most likely.

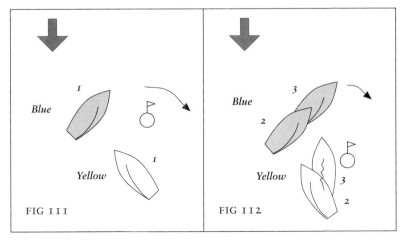

FIG 111

FIG 112

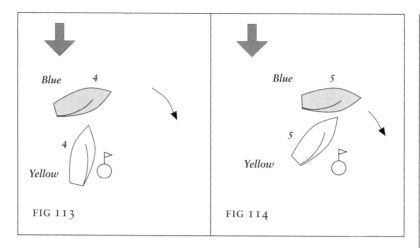

FIG 113   FIG 114

And all this happens in as little as 3 seconds. The umpires literally do not have time to call all the information that is required to decide the issue. In practice, a slightly pragmatic approach is required. Blue is first required to be crossing clear before Yellow luffs. Blue is also required to allow room for Yellow to luff head-to-wind, which in practice is enough room to round the mark. Yellow, while permitted to round inside, is required to do so in one continuous smooth turn and bear away promptly to a proper course. If she holds her head-to-wind course before tacking, luffed abnormally slowly, or leaves a large gap between herself and the mark then her luff was not 'rounding the mark' and infringed rule 35.

Port rounding

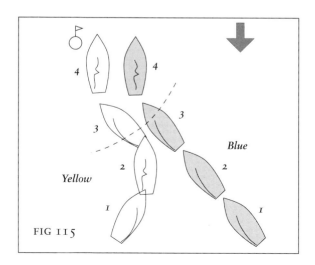

FIG 115

We move on now to Fig 115. Blue is approaching the mark close hauled on starboard tack and Yellow approaching close hauled on port tack. Yellow chooses to tack rather than have to make a large dip to clear the stern of Blue. Yellow completes her tack at position 3 and must do so giving Blue an opportunity to keep clear [rule 41.2]. Having done so Yellow becomes the right of way yacht [rule 37.1] and a new overlap begins.

Yellow is entitled to luff to round the mark, as she pleases, if Blue is behind mast abeam, or up to her proper course giving Blue an opportunity to respond, if Blue is ahead of mast abeam. It is important that Yellow was not 'clear astern' of Blue as Blue entered the two length circle (at the time they were not on the same tack and therefore the terms 'clear astern', 'clear ahead' and 'overlap' do not apply) as Yellow would then be required to keep clear while Blue rounds the mark.

Umpires must take care to observe that Yellow does in fact complete her tack and that Blue then has an opportunity to keep clear before Yellow luffs.

As Blue approaches the mark she would be wise to leave as little room for Yellow as possible. When Blue sees that Yellow might attempt to tack inside she should bear away to below the layline, relying on her boatspeed to enable her to shoot the mark. When Yellow sees Blue bear down she really must consider just bearing away and following Blue around the mark. She is bound to be close, have a little time on starboard tack to prepare her rounding properly and be in good shape to attack down the run.

8
Downwind

Because the leading yacht no longer has the ability to use her dirty air to hold back her opponent the greatest opportunities for changing the lead occur downwind. Downwind legs are frequently the most exciting of the course and the excitement has been enhanced with the adoption of downwind finishes.

Unless a particular downwind leg is the last, as is more and more common in match racing, there is a further opportunity for the yacht behind. Any reasonable inside overlap at the mark will often result in a change of leader. Leeward mark rounding will be covered in Chapter 9, but, as we have seen before, thinking ahead to what is to come plays a vital part in the current tactics.

This chapter will include reaches as well as runs, but first we need to take a look at some points that are common to all downwind legs.

Luffing downwind

We have covered in some detail the rules that apply to luffing matches, mast abeam, hailing and proper courses, so there is no need to repeat it all again. Remember though, that in anything like a breeze, a luffing match will cause the yachts to heel and the most likely point of contact is high up in the rigs. Indeed, if you are the yacht luffing it can be very effective suddenly to dump the sails thus bringing the boat upright sharply. The windward yacht is in real trouble. If they do the same, the spinnaker will foul, if they don't the rigs will hit. A further opportunity for the leeward yacht is to bear away sharply, either in response to a hail or whenever the yachts are very close. Contact will often result. If not, it is still worth a protest as the umpires may, possibly quite rightly, decide that the luff was terminated only to avoid otherwise inevitable contact.

Bearing away before contact also protects the leeward yacht from risk of infringing rule 32, damage, obliging her to attempt to avoid a collision resulting in damage (or serious damage, depending on the yachts being used).

Broaching

The most extreme case of heeling while luffing is of course the dreaded broach. While the yacht may well be out of control, there is no rule in the book that in any way protects a yacht that is out of control - even if this is as a result of breakdown - unless the yacht has first capsized. Broaching, by definition, involves luffing, and you would usually sail above a proper course; so if you broach without luffing rights and another yacht has to act to keep clear, then you infringe. The only consolation is that if you do have luffing rights, then in trying to keep clear, your opponent normally broaches too! Interestingly, if you can get the top of the mast into the water, even a wave top, you are now capsized according to rule 46.3. Until your masthead has cleared the water and you have regained steerage way your opponent is now required to keep clear. This is a fairly risky way to try to get your opponent to infringe and when tried too many times is likely to result in mutiny of your crew.

Spinnakers and spinnaker poles

Just a few points about spinnakers and the equipment used to set them. The rules no longer require the use of spinnaker poles. However, when in use, a spinnaker pole shall be attached to the foremost mast and only one pole may be in use at a time.

In practice the rule prohibits a crew member standing on the foredeck, with one end of the pole, pushing it out and effectively extending its length. It cannot be left for long with one end attached to the spinnaker or sheets without being attached to the mast.

Normally the pole is set up before rounding which in turn requires the decision to be made whether to gybe immediately or not. What is worse, once set up it is not easy to change your mind and it is easy for your opponent to predict what you will do and plan their rounding accordingly. Now the kite can be hoisted, set, gybed or not and then the pole attached. This is also a valuable option; if you have been forced to approach close to the windward mark without time to set the pole first, there is no need to delay hoisting in order to comply with any rule.

Rule 54, Propulsion

This section has been included in this chapter because it is when sailing downwind that most problems occur. The principles equally apply to infringements wherever they occur.

There are no special rules concerning what is allowed and what is prohibited so far as match racing is concerned. The sailing instructions should be examined, by both competitors and umpires, to see if class rules apply, and then to check the class rules for alteration of rule 54.3 (b), pumping on a free leg or not. The appendix does change the way that infringements are dealt with when umpires are used. First, it is only the umpires who can take any action (competitors are not permitted to protest against each other), and secondly, the penalty is the same as any other penalty in match racing.

When deciding whether particular actions of a yacht and her crew infringe the rule, the umpires should be certain before penalising. If they do decide to penalise they should approach the yacht close enough to shout 'Pumping' or 'Rocking' or whatever. The competitors may not like the decision, but at least they will understand why they are being penalised.

Although we have included this section in the downwind chapter it equally applies to any infringement on upwind legs.

Bearing away below a proper course

This is just a reminder, as it only affects free legs of the course, that rule 39 is amended by the match racing appendix. It only obliges a yacht not to sail below her proper course while an overlap exists and the leeward yacht is clearly less than two (rather than the normal three) lengths away. It places no such obligation, as does the normal rule, while clear ahead.

Reaching legs

For the purposes of this book we will define a reach as 'a free leg of the course, set such that the course is closer to the wind than a yacht would sail for best downwind speed made good'.

Using this definition means that unless the boats are overlapped, a reaching leg is a boatspeed leg. The problems of fleet racing, when each yacht gets higher and higher in order to maintain clear air, do not exist with only two yachts on the course. The yacht ahead, say Blue, should attempt to stay as near the rhumb-line as possible while Yellow should try to drag the race up to windward. The farther to windward the pair go the easier it will be for Yellow to blanket and hence roll over the top of Blue. If Yellow really succeeds, she will effectively turn the reach into a run and thus enhance the possibility of overtaking.

Should Yellow get close enough to affect the wind of her opponent, Blue will have to decide if, when and how much to luff. A short, sharp, well timed luff has a greater chance of resulting in an infringement by Yellow and will not take the boats so far to windward as a longer slower luff.

Reaching legs with cross tide

If a race takes place in a cross tide it is not possible, with just a windward and leeward mark, to set a perfect beat and a perfect run. At some time an uptide reaching leg must be set to achieve this. The distance of the offset is a function of both boatspeed and current. It follows that in light winds the offset can be quite large. The direction of the current, relative to the wind, will also determine which way the marks are to be rounded. If you are looking upwind and the current is from the left, the mark must be rounded to port. It is most usual to set the offset leg as a beam reach from the windward mark. It is not intended to be a spinnaker leg, but simply a dead leg of the course to get the boats in the correct position for the run. Spinnakers are normally prohibited by the sailing instructions until the 'wing' mark is rounded because of the risk of spinnaker damage when being set too close to the wind.

The run

As with the beat, it is the yacht behind that determines the tactics while the yacht in front is trying to protect her lead. The difference is that the yacht in front will often be satisfied with just maintaining a lead. She will also have to make the first choice; whether to go to the left – or the right hand side.

Fig 116 shows the downwind leg. Notice that when we talk about the left hand side or the right hand side, it means for the yachts, not these figures, which always have the wind blowing from the top of the page.

As there are laylines upwind, represented by the port and starboard close hauled courses, so there are laylines downwind. They represent the course the yachts will sail in order to get to the leeward mark in the shortest possible time. This is known as sailing the best VMG course. Sailing to best VMG requires practice to judge the angle - more so than sailing the best upwind course when tell-tales on the sails are helpful. While there are many instruments available that will directly show VMG, most match racing events prohibit the use of such instruments. This is to reduce the cost of match race boats and to eliminate the need to calibrate equally the instruments - both headaches for organisers providing yachts.

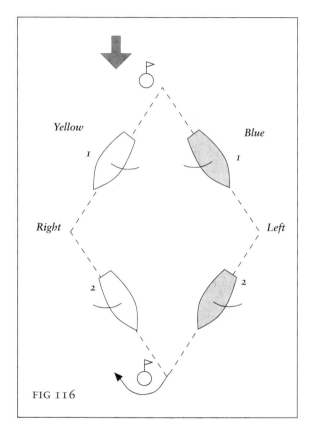

FIG 116

While, as we have said before, this is not a boatspeed book, understanding these laylines and best VMG is absolutely vital downwind. Every type of boat is different, but for any boat it pays to sail lower (nearer dead downwind) in the gusts and stronger winds. Watch out though for the boats, normally older designs, that sail downwind fastest by the lee.

Let's assume that Blue starts off on port tack, sailing to the left of the run and gybes at the correct point to approach the leeward mark on starboard tack. Yellow takes the right hand side of the course, starboard first then port, both as in Fig 116.

When the leeward mark is to be rounded to starboard, Blue will have the benefit of starboard tack but will be outside boat. (We look at the interaction of these two in Chapter 9). When the leeward mark is to be rounded to port, Blue has the benefit of the starboard approach and being the inside yacht. When it is a run to the finish these considerations are of less importance unless the line is so biased that effectively one end or the other is a rounding mark.

Yet again the starboard rounding is not as clear cut as port.

Blanketing

Blanketing is the downwind equivalent of close cover, only this time all the benefits are for the yacht astern. Again boat types are different but most will affect the wind for about ten lengths to leeward. However, blanketing is normally effective up to about four boat lengths away in the time span that is available during most matches.

Assuming Blue to be in front her first objective whenever Yellow is within blanketing range is to get away from the windward mark as fast as possible - every inch of distance she can gain could be vital. Similarly, Yellow will try to close the gap.

Next it is important to recall the difference we found before the start when being forced either to the left or to the right. It is much easier to escape gybing on to starboard than it is to escape gybing on to port. This means that early on Blue is safer running on port tack than on starboard tack. If the marks are to starboard this means a bear away set and to keep going finding that best VMG as soon as possible. If rounding the windward mark to port you will be on starboard tack and therefore looking for the opportunity to gybe. Yellow, rounding close behind, will attempt to bear away faster to 'get down inside' in order to prevent the gybe. These positions are shown in Figs 117 and 118.

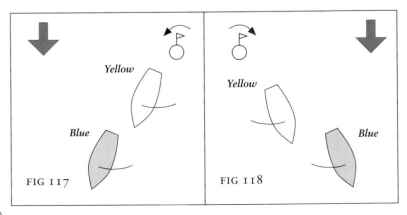

FIG 117   FIG 118

There are a few consolations for Blue, and she should be aware of these if she is to maintain her lead to the leeward mark.

In order to get past, Yellow will normally have to go to windward. This puts her at risk of being luffed, so she dare not stay too close. The farther she goes to windward, the higher she must go of the layline (provided that Blue has got it right). If she goes far enough to avoid the risk of the luff totally, then Blue simply gybes to the other layline - maintaining best progress to the leeward mark. Yellow not only sails too far, but turns the boat too much.

If Yellow succeeds in passing, but too early, then Blue will have the opportunity to reverse the blanket. If she is too late on the outside for the next mark, it will all be to no avail.

On all but the finishing leg, then, it is most common for Yellow to concentrate on obtaining a good inside overlap at the next mark and for Blue to defend her clear ahead or inside position.

Windshifts

Similar to the beat, windshifts are of greater importance when the yachts are farther apart. First look at Figs 119 and 120 to see

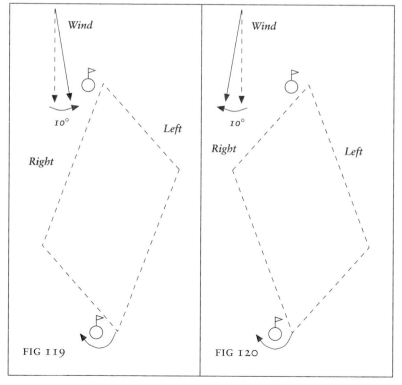

FIG 119   FIG 120

the effect on the laylines of a wind other than straight up and down the course.

If the wind is steady then the distance sailed to get to the leeward mark is the same whichever layline is sailed. In the absence of any competition, current, wind shear across the course or any other reason you might think of, it is best to sail the longest of the two tacks first. This is simply because it takes you more directly to the mark and it is then easier to judge accurately the layline to the mark. The classical way to predict which way this will be is to monitor your time on each tack going upwind. If you spent most time on starboard tack upwind, you will set off on port tack downwind and vice versa.

The terminology of left, right, headers, lifts, backs and veers can be even more confusing downwind. Let us try to sort it out. A left shift is always a shift which, when looking upwind, comes more from the left than it was before. This is always the same as a wind that is backing. A backing (left hand) shift always lifts you on port tack and heads you on starboard tack irrespective of whether you are beating, reaching or running.

Conversely, a right hand shift is a veer and always lifts you on starboard tack.

Where the run is different from the beat is that whereas you tack on headers on the beat, you gybe on lifts on the run. If the wind goes left you are lifted while on port tack and you ought to gybe. To gybe from port to starboard, you turn right.

Another way to picture this is to imagine that you are sailing on your VMG layline on port tack, heading directly for the mark. If you do not change your course but the wind changes suddenly a long way to the left (anticlockwise), you will automatically gybe and still be pointing to the mark!

Our golden rule survives: if you expect a shift to the left, go left. If you expect a shift to the right, go right. In both cases the yacht farther to the left or right will gain most, provided they don't go outside the laylines.

Covering

As we have seen, the term 'covering' is hardly appropriate when your opponent is a couple of boat lengths behind you sitting on your wind. However, should you be a clear distance ahead, then you certainly do need to cover your opponent's every move. To cover, you simply stay between your opponent and the next mark, or finishing line, while always sailing at your best VMG, and if in any doubt as to which side to be at any one time then protect the inside berth. In the event of a large lead, and especially in light airs when the yacht behind can make enormous gains bringing up fresh breeze from astern, you will first need to set off on your chosen tack. When you are as far from the mark as your oppponent has to sail to get to it, gybe. That way you should be dead downwind as he rounds and in a position to cover whichever way he goes.

Yachts on different legs

Unless both yachts go round the mark together, there will be a period when the two yachts are on different legs of the course. As it is easier for a yacht on a beat to cause problems for a yacht on the run than vice versa, and the leader is less likely to be looking for trouble, the issue of yachts on different legs most frequently arises just after the leader has rounded the windward mark.

In addition to the basic rules there is an additional rule (Appendix B6 rule 1.4(a) which, unless sailing a proper course, prohibits a yacht from 'acting to interfere with a yacht on another leg of the course'. We discussed the term 'acting to interfere' in Chapter 2, but it is worth amplification here and some examples. Many skippers are concerned on reading this rule that even a right of way yacht must keep out of the way of a yacht on another leg of the course. There is no such requirement.

There is a good deal of difference between the expression 'to act such that a yacht happens to interfere...' and the expression 'to act to interfere'.

If Yellow, still on the beat, tacks on to starboard, has never been outside the laylines, and holds a steady close hauled course, and Blue has to alter course to fulfil her obligation to keep clear, Yellow does not 'act to interfere', nor does she deviate from a proper course, and therefore does not infringe.

If, however, Yellow goes clearly beyond the layline, or bears away after tacking, or even tacks a number of times in quick succession when she has previously tacked infrequently, then she could have 'acted to interfere' and deviated from a proper course. Blue should protest.

Blue must keep a look out for Yellow as she rounds the mark and be prepared to sail high to keep out of trouble. It is, of course, an advantage to be running on starboard!

Gybing at the layline

Whenever Yellow achieves the inside position as in Figs 117 and 118, she is quite happy to go beyond the layline. The further they go past, when they eventually gybe, the more likely it is that Yellow will then be in front - even if they have to beat back to the mark!

This is shown in Fig 121, which is equally appropriate for either gybe and either mark rounding. At position 1, before either have reached the layline, Blue is actually nearer the mark. If both were to gybe, she would be right of way, leeward. She will be inside yacht if marks are to be rounded to starboard, and by using her luffing rights she will have a good chance of breaking the overlap if the mark is to be rounded to port. If only it were safe for her to gybe!

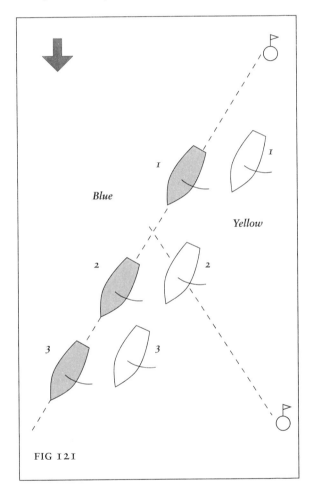

FIG 121

By the time the yachts have progressed to position 2, the situation is already worse for Blue. If both gybe, Yellow has a much better chance of attaining mast abeam. Blue will not be able to luff so effectively as they are already sailing much higher and Yellow is probably closer to the mark.

Should they go all the way to position 3, it becomes quite clear that Yellow is closer to the mark, and by a sufficient margin that if they both gybe here and head directly to the mark, Yellow will be clear ahead and be able to round the mark either way without difficulty.

It is important then to see what are the obligations on each yacht as the laylines are approached.

There are three possibilities; these are shown in Figs 122, 123 and 124.

In 122, Yellow is clear astern of Blue and is therefore obliged to keep clear. Blue, on the other hand, cannot gybe unless she keeps clear while doing so and when she is on port tack.

In Fig 123, there is no doubt that, although there is an overlap, Blue is ahead of mast abeam. This is typical of the situation when Yellow has established her overlap from clear astern. Blue is required to keep clear, but Yellow does not have luffing rights. Yellow may not sail above her proper course, which she will do if she sails beyond the layline. If her only way to sail a proper course is to gybe first, then she must do so.

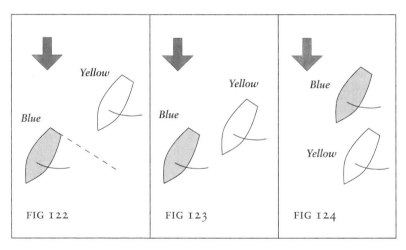

FIG 122   FIG 123   FIG 124

Fig 124 is not quite so obvious at it might seem. It depends on what has happened previously to determine if Yellow has luffing rights or not. If she has come from astern and never been clear ahead, then she does not have luffing rights and the situation is the same as in Fig 123. If, however, during the overlap Blue has never been ahead of mast abeam then Yellow has the right to luff as she pleases or to continue to sail on as far as she likes or until Blue does achieve mast abeam.

In Fig 124, had Yellow come from clear astern, it may be possible for her to gybe, twice, and still have Blue behind mast abeam on the completion of her second gybe. Yellow must keep clear while doing so, but by pulling the mainboom almost to the centreline she could complete two gybes very quickly (providing that the mainsail fills on each tack) with virtually no alteration of course or risk of fouling Blue with her boom. On completion a new overlap exists and therefore she will have established luffing rights and thus avoid the requirement to gybe at the layline.

If Blue is faced with the situation in Fig 122, she only has to bear away to give an overlap to Yellow - who will then be obliged to sail her proper course. Blue should wait until it is clear that the layline has been reached, bear away to give the overlap, wait a couple of seconds and, if there is no reaction from Yellow, immediately display code flag Y to protest. She should not shout out any warnings.

Similarly when Blue is sure the layline in Fig 123 has been reached, she should protest without warning.

To see how umpires decide such a case, it is useful to refer back to Fig 121. Any call that involves proper course is notoriously difficult because it is subjective. All the time they are on the race course on a particular day the umpires must observe yachts that are racing. What angle do they sail at? How consistent are they? How does wind speed and current vary across the course? How does this affect the course that they sail? All this information is vital when the time comes to make the judgement: is that yacht, at this moment in time, sailing a proper course, or above, or below?

In practice, there will be a range of courses that comply with a reasonable view of 'proper course', despite the fact that there might be one perfect course. The umpires should discuss this between themselves - frequently if the conditions are changing. By doing so it is surprising how much agreement there is, which is encouraging for the confidence in one's decision making ability.

Establishing a good idea of proper course, when yachts are *not* influencing each other, will prepare the umpires well. As the yachts sail down the run the umpires will be discussing the options each has, in order to anticipate any incident. At about position 1 in Fig 121 - that is, well before the laylines are reached by either yacht - the umpires should begin to address the specific issue. One would say 'I'm not near the layline yet, do you agree?' This process goes on until the umpire assigned to Yellow says, 'I'm getting close...I'm there now...Do you agree?' The other umpire might reply, 'There could be doubt...What about cross current?...What about that puff of wind over there?' This will continue until both agree that without any doubt Yellow is over the layline. Her umpire should then say, 'If Blue protests now I'd penalise Yellow...agree?' 'Yes' the other responds.

If Blue protests before this final agreement is reached, there would be no penalty.

It is quite hopeless for umpires to wait until they see a protest flag, wonder what it is all about, *then* start to address the issue. Time has passed since the flag was displayed, and the flag means 'I'm alleging she *has* infringed'. It does not mean, 'I think she is *about* to infringe'. If the yachts have already gybed a few times down the run, they might be no more than a few boat lengths from the mark. The yachts then travel from position 1 to 2 to 3 with alarming rapidity.

Continuing obstructions downwind

Not every venue has the luxury of an unobstructed place to race. Mind you, not every venue has the Statue of Liberty to race around either. It was there that we both came across continuing obstructions downwind for the first time while umpiring. It was 1988 at the Liberty Cup. The Hudson River was ebbing at up to 3 knots, the winds were light, and the boats were 28 ft (8.5 m) long, not very fast. The need to get out of the current was paramount and one pair after another headed for Liberty Island. The shoreline was a bit like that in Fig 125, with bits that stuck out, but remained cleverly hidden under not-too-clear water.

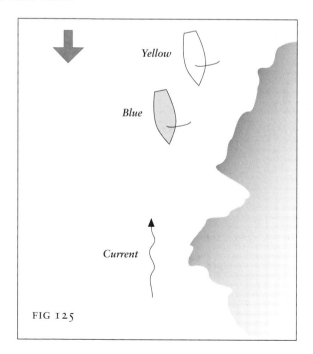

FIG 125

Blue was clear ahead and presumably trying to get as close to the shore as possible. Yellow went even farther inshore and, with the combination of less current and some blanketing, she closed up. Eventually she gained an inside overlap, but soon after Blue protested. The umpires were close, but still had absolutely no idea how deep the water was, so how should the situation be judged? Well, the clue is in the rule - in this case 42.3(b): '...and a yacht *clear astern* may establish an *overlap* between a yacht *clear ahead* and the *obstruction*, provided, at that time, there is *room* for her to pass in safety.'

The first important issue is, did Yellow establish an overlap? Then, when the overlap has been established the umpires must look ahead to see where Yellow must sail in order to pass between Blue and the obstruction, assuming that Blue does not move any farther (see the phrase in the rule 'at that time'). If Yellow sails in the identified area without problem, she did not infringe, and Blue must now give her room for any part of the obstruction that may require them to sail farther offshore. When judging this, the umpires must remember that Blue's boom is no longer in the way: they must imagine it is.

If Yellow runs aground, or sails farther from the shore than at the time she established the overlap, before she reaches the point where she would have passed Blue, had Blue not moved, then Yellow infringed, and her infringement was establishing the overlap.

This is one of the few times when the umpires have to wait to see what happens before they can decide the case. It must also be one of the most difficult decisions to have to make. If there is doubt (would Yellow have passed Blue's boom?), the umpires have a real dilemma. Penalising Yellow favours safety and the protection of the yachts (probably provided by the organisers), but goes against the principle of only penalising when certain.

The difficulty can be almost eliminated if the race organisers lay a line of marks along such an obstruction. The sailing instructions need to include a clause to the effect that the line of marks is the line of safe pilotage. Some judgement remains but it is much easier to work to this line than to be required to guess how deep the water is. This system has been successfully used at Lymington.

9
Leeward marks

We have included in this chapter all marks except windward marks. There are no special rules that apply to one type of leeward mark or another; we have simply used the different versions to demonstrate different aspects of the rules and tactics as seems most appropriate. The important difference between a leeward mark and a windward mark is that the boats do not approach on a beat, and therefore rule 42 always has to be considered irrespective of the yachts being on the same tack or not.

It must also be remembered that once the yachts are 'about to round', rule 42 applies and will override conflicting basic rules. Also, the definitions 'clear astern', 'clear ahead' and 'overlap' apply to the yachts, even when on opposite tacks.

The objectives of rounding a leeward mark must be to ensure that you only give room when required to do so and that you take it when you are entitled to do so. In addition, it is most important to round the mark in the most efficient manner - which means not just rounding close, but maintaining boatspeed and position. Gaining a fraction of a length during your rounding manoeuvre may make the difference in establishing an overlap at the next mark or being able to cross your opponent on the next tack.

Gybe or Wing marks

As the reach in a match race tends to be about boatspeed the approaches to a gybe mark are straightforward enough. The only significant chance of a gain or loss is when the yacht that would otherwise be astern manages to establish an overlap and thus forces her opponent to round on the outside.

Figs 126 and 127 show the two yachts approaching the gybe mark on starboard tack. In Fig 126, at position 1, Yellow is clearly overlapped, but Blue picks up a wave and as she enters the two length circle the overlap is in doubt. This is one of the cases when the normal rules place an onus. If Blue denies room and Yellow protests, then Blue would have to satisfy the protest committee that she broke the overlap outside the two length circle. While this onus clause cannot be applied as it stands when umpires are used, umpires will decide in a similar manner. If it was clear that Yellow at one time had an overlap, then that overlap exists until the umpires are certain that it does not; and if they are in doubt about when the overlap was broken, then it was too late.

Fig 127 is similar, but this time the onus is on the inside yacht. It is clear that Yellow does not have an overlap at position 1, while position 2 is identical to position 2 in Fig 126. Now all the doubts favour Blue, and unless the umpires are certain, then the overlap was not established in time to give Yellow right to room around the mark.

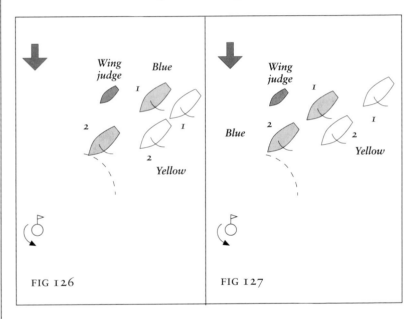

FIG 126   FIG 127

The wing judge boat is shown in position to make these calls. It is important to note that the judge sits at approximately the *three* boat length circle, which will probably look like the two length circle to the crews of the yachts as they will tend to foreshorten the distance they are from the mark. One judge in the boat should be looking to judge when the outside yacht, or the yacht clear ahead, enters the two length circle. The other judge will be looking for the overlap: carefully watching for the spinnaker of one over the transom of the other.

If the wing boat judges are using hand signals to communicate to the umpire boat, which should be following looking down the gap between the two yachts, the arm will be raised while there is an overlap and the arm held horizontal when the overlap is broken. Arm down means that the wing boat is out of position and thus cannot make a call or they think the issue is so clear that no signals are required. It is helpful if the arm is waved, either horizontal or above the head, as the two length circle is called.

Competitors use these signals at their own risk! They cannot claim redress if, for instance, no overlap is signalled, and Yellow luffs out and hits Blue.

It is obviously vital that crews understand the way these situations are handled. Generally it is much easier to use the rule as intended with umpires, than it ever is with normal hearings. Unless you get a witness the onus provisions are very onerous indeed; and it is rare that you have time to decide if you have a good witness, before you make the decision to go for room. Our advice to skippers when umpires are used is as follows:

- Skippers have to live on their ability to judge distances, overlaps and the like.

- If you are sure you have an overlap, go for it.

- If you are sure you have broken the overlap, deny room.

- If you are in doubt, bail out or give room. You can still protest and as long as your judgement is good you shouldn't be penalised.

- If your judgement is lousy, learn to improve it.

Fig 128 shows a situation that is very similar to that in Figs 121 to 124, gybing at the layline. This time it is a mark that causes the gybe, rather than the layline.

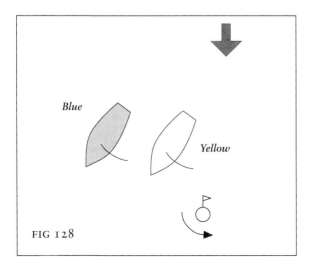

FIG 128

There is no doubt that Yellow to leeward is the right of way yacht and therefore has the right to sail her proper course. If she has luffing rights, then she may still luff as she pleases. If she does not have luffing rights, rule 42.1(e) obliges her to gybe at the first reasonable opportunity, when a gybe is required in order to most directly assume a proper course to the next mark, as in this case.

Breaking an overlap

Fig 129 shows Blue and Yellow approaching a downwind mark to be rounded to port (starboard would be the same, but mirrored).Yellow is overlapped until Blue luffs at position 3 to become clear ahead, just before entering the two length circle. Yellow really does have to be quite careful as, when Blue bears away again, she could find it very difficult to go round the outside.

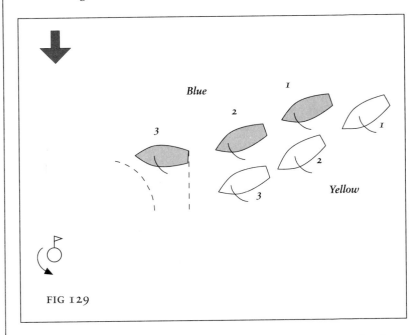

FIG 129

There is an overriding rule (42.3(i)) that limits a yacht from claiming room when establishing an overlap from astern if the outside yacht is unable to give the room (even if established outside the two length circle). There is no such protection for a yacht denied room at the last second. In order to avoid the possibility of having to gybe inside the mark, Yellow should luff as soon as Blue does. She may not preserve her overlap, but at least she will not be in dire straits.

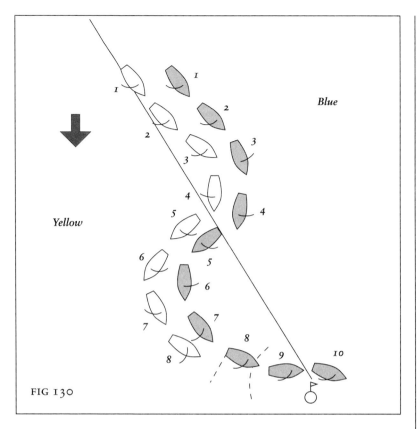

FIG 130

Fig 130, at position 1 shows Yellow on the layline, to a starboard mark, with an overlap on Blue. If Blue doesn't break the overlap she is fairly certain to be trailing up the beat. At position 2 Blue luffs to create some space for a gybe. Yellow cannot luff too far to follow without infringing rule 39, as Blue is ahead of mast abeam, even if Blue does not need to respond. Blue gybes on to starboard and Yellow has to respond to the new obligation. Yellow gybes at position 5 and then, as windward boat, has to luff to keep clear. At position 6, Blue bears away and gybes to position 7. Yellow tries to do the same, but is on the outside of a circle and cannot maintain the overlap.

The previous scenario, although complex and requiring good timing from Blue, does give a key as to how to approach a starboard hand leeward mark from the left hand side of the course, when your opponent is close behind.

Fig 131 shows that if Blue simply sails all the way down the port tack layline and then gybes to sail the starboard tack layline it is relatively easy for Yellow to gybe onto her weather side and use her blanket to obtain an inside overlap. Blue has two alternatives: she can sail this course and then luff Yellow up to the solid starboard line. Provided that Yellow does not succeed in sailing right over the top of her into a clear ahead position, Blue gybes at position 2 back to the mark. This is virtually the same position as 5 in Fig 130. When Blue gybes, Yellow is unlikely to obtain an inside overlap and Blue will succeed in rounding first. As a slight variation, if Blue gybed at position 1, before the layline to the mark, she reduces the need to luff, which always carries the risk of being sailed over as Yellow sails around a smaller circle.

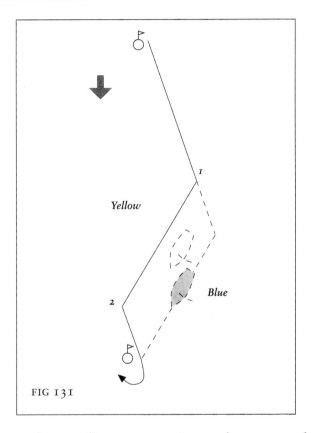

FIG 131

Starboard rounding - opposite tack approach

Fig 132 shows Blue approaching the leeward mark on starboard tack. The positions of Yellow are not a course followed by her but three alternative approach lines on port tack. Each alternative shows the position at which one of the yachts will have to do something if contact is to be avoided.

Rule 36, Opposite tacks - basic rule, requires Yellow to keep clear. Rule 42, provided that Yellow has an overlap at two lengths as in these cases, requires Blue to give sufficient room for Yellow to round in a seamanlike manner, including room for her to gybe. Clearly these two are in conflict, which means that from the time that rule 42 applies it overrides rule 36. However, should Yellow take more room than she needs to round in a seamanlike manner, she will infringe. She will not infringe rule 42, which places no obligation on her to round in a seamanlike manner, but she will infringe either rule 36 (before she gybes), rule 41 (while gybing), or rule 37 (after gybing) because these rules are only overridden to the extent that they conflict.

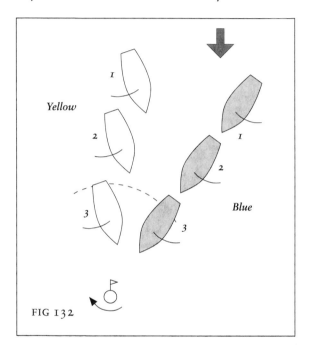

FIG 132

In practice, Yellow will be given the benefit of the doubt provided that she remains as close to the mark as is reasonable in the prevailing conditions. She will not be afforded the luxury, though, of a wide entry to the mark in order to achieve a tight exit.

Rule 42 starts to apply when the yachts are 'about to round' - a phrase that we discussed, in some detail, in Chapter 2 and established that the distance from the mark will vary according to the conditions and the yachts. At position 1, Yellow will certainly be required to respond. Even if the conditions were such that the yachts were about to round, the course that Yellow is sailing would result in her taking more room than she is entitled to take and her basic obligation under rule 36 remains.

At position 2, close to entering the two length circle, the yachts will almost certainly be about to round (unless light winds and adverse current). Yellow must make sure that she doesn't enter the rounding too wide and Blue must allow room for Yellow to gybe. When the rules work in this way, placing an obligation on both yachts, marginal calls will be required from the umpires. Both yachts should recognise that by forcing the issue they are both taking a risk.

By position 3 the situation is resolved: Blue must give room, and Yellow must not take more room than entitled.

If Blue is a little farther ahead, although she will still be required to give Yellow room, it is usual for her to be able to break clear ahead while Yellow completes her gybe, at which time she may luff hard to round the mark as close as possible.

Before Blue enters the two length circle she should attempt to break the overlap by bearing away. If the yachts are sailing to large gybing angles this is quite difficult and as most skippers think they are at the two length circle when they are in fact nearer four lengths away, it is frequently misjudged. As Blue luffs to round the mark she has to be very careful not to give a late overlap to Yellow.

The rounding path

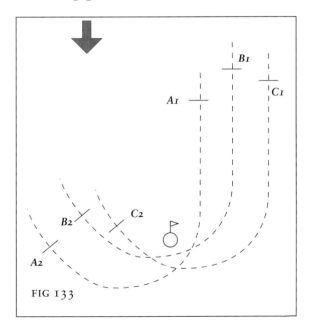

FIG 133

Fig 133 shows the tracks of three leeward mark roundings: A, B and C. There are many variations on these tracks, including the angle of approach and the speed of the turn (which may be initially slow), but it is important that we compare like with like. Each has been carefully drawn using the same template and the positions 1 and 2 marked at identical points, also from the template. Each passes the mark at the same distance, but in A the mark is passed with the wind aft, in B the wind is abeam, and in C the yacht is close hauled.

In terms of the most efficient rounding, track B is the best, C next and A is worst. That A is worst holds few surprises, but many skippers would have said that to exit from the mark already close hauled is the best. It may well be if you have your opponent directly in front of you and every inch gained to windward is important, but if you round in front, or even well behind, track B will save you distance. Another way to look at the figure is to imagine the mark moved to the same position for track C as it is for B. It will now be farther from the windward mark than it was. The effect of track C is to lengthen the run by a quarter to half a boat length, depending on the yachts and conditions.

If you are in the lead and your opponent is close behind, track B is even more important. It means that should he tack immediately on rounding the mark, you can tack at exactly the same time a safer distance to windward and consequently start any duel exactly in phase. Should he choose not to tack, your safe leeward position will soon have its effect.

10
The finish

The objective at the finishing line is quite simple: to get there first! Most matches will by now be effectively over, and the leader only has to sail sensibly and conservatively to cross the line, well away from any marks, and win the race. However, if the race is close then there is everything to play for and this chapter becomes the most important one in the book.

Essentially there are only two kinds of finishes, upwind and downwind, with the latter becoming more popular. In either case the finishing line is normally the same line as the starting line. This avoids the need for two committee boats, but an upwind finish requires the line to be set between the leeward and windward mark, usually half way up the beat.

The advantages of a downwind finish are seen to be that:

- there are more close finishes, increasing spectator enjoyment

- spinnakers, often with sponsors logos are flying at the finish

- a longer first beat

- yachts not racing, either before or after finishing, can sail around to leeward of the whole course out of the way of yachts racing yet close to the committee boat.

- Spectators can get close to the action with less interference.

Judging the finishing line bias

With either an upwind or a downwind finish it is equally important to judge the finishing line bias in order to avoid sailing farther than necessary. A 5 degree bias on an upwind finishing line that is eight lengths long results in a difference of one boat length in distance sailed to either end (with a 90 degree tacking angle) (Fig 134).

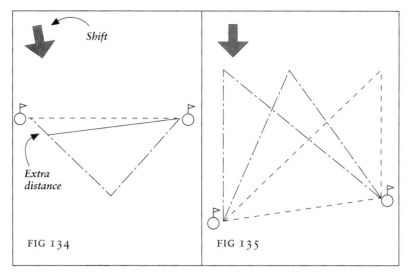

FIG 134

Shift

Extra distance

FIG 135

Fig 135, on the other hand, shows that the effect of bias on a downwind finish cannot be determined without knowing the position of the yachts. Once over the laylines, whenever they are on the right hand side, the right hand mark will be the nearer unless the bias is excessive. This means that in order to take advantage of any bias you have to know what the bias is much earlier than with an upwind finish.

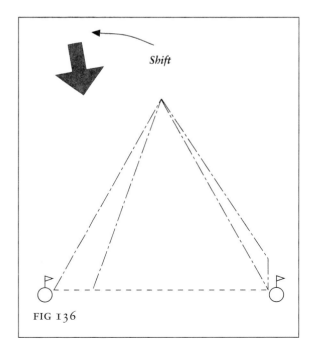

Shift

FIG 136

With downwind finishes the starting line becomes the finishing line. It is unusual for the pin end mark to be moved while a flight is in progress. It is important therefore to know the wind direction and line bias at the start. By checking the wind direction on the last leg it should be possible to work out the finishing line bias in good time. As Figs 134 and 136 show, the more the wind shifts to the left the more the right hand end will be favoured, irrespective of whether the finish is upwind or downwind. If possible, the bias should be known before the start of the last leg when the tactical planning must take place.

Finishing upwind

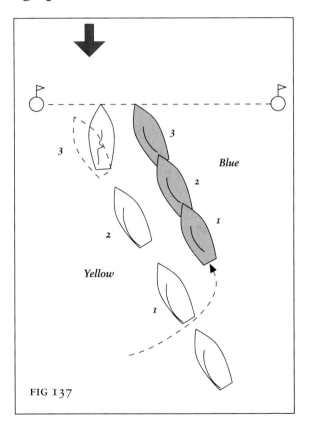

FIG 137

In Fig 137 Yellow is approaching the finishing line. Blue has just crossed ahead and tacked to windward and into a position ahead of mast abeam. Yellow is sailing faster as Blue is still accelerating out of her tack. Yellow does not have luffing rights, but a proper course for her is to luff to hit the line as soon as she can. So her luff, even up to head-to-wind, does not infringe. Blue must keep clear. Even if Blue finishes first she is still subject to penalty if she infringes while straddling the line. Blue's defence, of course, is to luff first.

Most experienced crews on larger match racing yachts put a man on the bow to signal to the skipper when to luff for the finish. Wise crews practise every time they finish to windward. A luff too late can lose half a second, which might be the difference between winning and losing; a luff too early can leave the yacht head-to-wind to leeward of the finishing line - not a comfortable position.

In addition to the luff to finish, it is also common practice to drop the genoa at the same time to reduce the resistance as much as possible. It works well in yachts that carry their way, such as the Twelve Metres, but increases the penalty to be paid for getting it wrong.

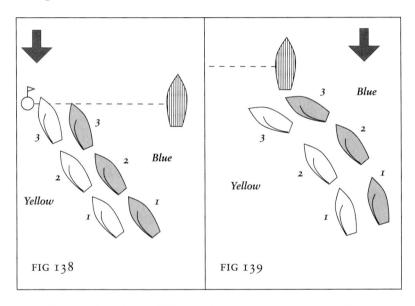

FIG 138   FIG 139

In Fig 138 there is no difference between the pin end mark and any port hand windward mark. Yellow may luff to pass the mark on the required side, with or without luffing rights. If she has luffing rights, she should probably luff earlier than in the figure in order to make some space for safety.

In Fig 139, again there is no difference to a windward mark, but this time a starboard hand one. At position 1, Yellow may luff as she pleases in the hope of either a penalty or breaking the overlap as she bears away. At position 2 they become about to round and now Yellow must give room to Blue. Blue should not hail for room. There is no requirement for her to do so and Yellow may deny her room in error, believing the situation to be similar to a starting mark. Yellow would then be certain to be penalised if Blue protests.

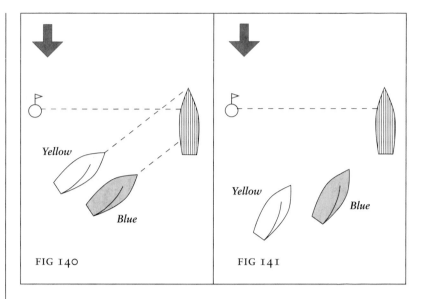

FIG 140   FIG 141

Approaching the committee boat, as in Figs 140 and 141, Blue, unlike at a starting mark, has the right to hail for room to tack. Her hail places an obligation on Yellow to do one of three things:

- ■ She can tack

- ■ she can hail 'You tack', or

- ■ as the obstruction is also a mark and if she thinks she can fetch the mark, she can hail something like 'Fetching' or 'Refused' (there is no specified hail in rule 43.3(b)).

Tactically, it is very important for Yellow to have decided earlier what her response is going to be. She will need to be sure exactly where the line is on the committee boat. As shown, it is somewhere towards the bow, but it could be anywhere – and not necessarily where it was at the start.

If she is in the position shown in Fig 140, such that she can tack immediately and still cross the line first, she should do so. Her tack does not have to be hurried: a good smooth one and the match is won.

If she needs a little more time and there is any room at all between her and Blue, she should immediately hail 'You tack' and delay her own tack as long as possible without risking fouling Blue. Remember when doing this that if sailing at 4 knots, only one second delay will take Yellow 6 ft (2 m) nearer the line. Her problem is that if Blue then puts in a very fast tack she must be prepared to respond. She should complete her tack, keeping clear and then immediately luff hard for the line.

If she is in the position of Fig 141, she will lose the match if she tacks. Her only chance to win the match is to refuse to tack. Should Yellow fetch the committee boat she has a chance of winning, if she doesn't fetch she will almost certainly lose following a protest from Blue. Once the room to tack is refused, Blue should just luff, head-to-wind if necessary and she will almost certainly cross the line first. Blue's win will now depend on her ability to avoid the mark. Should Blue pass beyond head-to-wind then Yellow can tack away, protest and win the match following the penalty on Blue.

Finishing downwind

There are no surprises in the rules at the downwind finish marks. Generally, they are much the same as those that apply at leeward marks. As with the upwind finish, it pays considerably to use your boatspeed to cross the line at right angles in the last boat length as do Yellow and Blue in Fig 142.

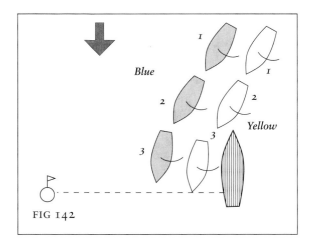

FIG 142

If Yellow has the choice earlier on the run, she is much more likely to win by establishing a leeward overlap than attempting to roll over Blue to windward. Remember that if you are on the left of the run the left hand mark will be the nearer (once beyond the layline to the farther end). If you can force your opponent from the left hand side towards the right you must benefit, both from the extra distance she will be forced to sail and from being able to bear away first for the line.

If the yachts are near the outer distance mark then Yellow will be required to give room to Blue, but she will be able to bear away for the line first and gain an advantage.

If the yachts approach the end of the line to be passed to starboard (normally the outer distance) on opposite tacks then the scenario is exactly the same as for starboard rounding of a leeward mark (described in full in Chapter 9, Fig 133)

If Yellow attempts to pass to windward, Blue should luff - but not violently unless certain of forcing Yellow to infringe (Fig 143). Blue is trying to keep Yellow trapped to windward until she crosses the Fig 143 layline on port tack to the committee boat end. Should Yellow get so far forward that she is blanketing Blue's wind despite sailing high, then Blue should gybe before losing boat speed. Should Yellow fall clear astern so that she is clear to gybe herself for the committee boat then Blue must also gybe immediately. If Yellow achieves mast abeam Blue will then be required to gybe unless the distance to the pin end is similar or less than the distance to the committee boat (sailing to the pin end is then Blue's proper course).

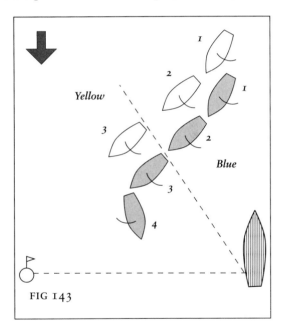

FIG 143

As the yachts will finish with spinnakers set, it will probably be the spinnakers that cross the line first. Provided they are in their normal position it is the spinnakers that count. There is nothing to prevent them from being set as far forward as they would normally be set: the halyard must be fully hoisted and the spinnaker drawing. It is not an infringement to fly the spinnaker further forward than normal but the yacht will not finish until the first part of the yacht in its normal position crosses the line, presumably the bow.

11

Protesting, seeking redress and hearings

The nature of match racing, as we have seen, is that the rules and the use of the rules are an integral part of the game, including manoeuvring your opponent into an infringement. This infringement results in a penalty following a protest. The protest itself has to follow certain rules which are again contained in Appendix B6. Protests are also used to allege other infringements and claims for redress whenever it is alleged that the fairness of the match has been prejudiced.

The Y flag protest

The Y flag protest is used only when umpires are appointed to the match and is an allegation by one yacht that another has infringed one of the rules that apply when yachts meet (sections B or C of Part IV of the IYRR). It must be displayed conspicuously, and it must be displayed very soon after the incident.

Once the Y flag is displayed the umpires are required to make a decision. The process is now irrevocably in progress and the umpires' decision is normally given within a few seconds. They may either 'green flag' the incident - award no penalty, or penalise the protested yacht. (The actual penalties were covered in Chapter 3.)

Once the umpires have signalled their decision, the Y flag must be lowered. A penalty initiated by the umpires may follow for failure to comply.

One of the difficulties is what to do if there is a second incident while you still have your Y flag displayed from the first incident. Almost all you can do is either to point to the flag or wave it about and trust that the umpires are alert. In these situations, the umpires' signals can be confusing. Suppose they rule no infringement for the first flag and a penalty for the second. Theoretically, they should first display a green flag followed by a penalty signal. The other yacht may not be aware that a second protest flag has been displayed, so on seeing the first signal will carry on without looking back to see the penalty call.

A similar technicality arises when both yachts display a Y flag for the same incident. Should the umpires decide that neither has infringed then a green flag answers both Y flags. However when they decide to penalise one yacht, say Blue, and display her penalty signal, this cannot relate to Blue's protest flag as only the protested yacht may be penalised. Theoretically a green flag should be displayed in response to Blue's protest flag to say that Yellow has not infringed.

It is common practice that the green signal is omitted in these situations to avoid confusion.

What happens if the Y flag is lowered before the umpires have signalled their decision? Well, as we have said, the decision making process is irrevocably in progress, and Appendix B6 para 5.2 requires the umpires to decide as soon as possible after the display of the Y flag.

Should the Y flag not be lowered after the umpires' decision has been sigalled, then the yacht may infringe Appendix B6 para 5.3.

However this is not necessarily so. The umpires would need to be sure that there is no other incident for which the yacht is protesting of which they may be unaware. To check this they should display a green flag (with a sound signal as must accompany all umpire signals) a little while after any previous signal. If the Y flag remains displayed then it is time to penalise.

There can be no appeals, requests for redress or reopening of hearings from decisions made resulting from Y flag protests, or proceedings of any kind in relation to any action or non-action by umpires; they are all specifically excluded by the Appendix in para 8.1 and 8.2.

Yachts should protest whenever they believe that the other yacht may have infringed, but they should be wary of trying to get a decision when a protest is unwarranted. Although unlikely the first time, the umpires may deem such behaviour as unsportsmanlike and initiate a penalty themselves.

Red flag (code B) protests

A red flag protest by a yacht alleges an infringement of rules, including sailing instructions and rules of inspection, but excluding those for which the Y flag is applicable and those that are only initiated by umpires.

The flag must be flown as soon as possible after the incident or as soon as the protestor is aware of the facts justifying her protest, and the other yacht must be informed, just as under the usual rules.

No immediate decision is made, but umpires, on seeing a red flag displayed, should immediately look for evidence that may justify the protest. At the end of the race the umpires will approach the yacht and enquire why the flag has been flown. They may ask some questions at this time, but only to ensure they understand the issue. The chief umpire will then be informed and the umpires will decide which is the most appropriate way to handle the case.

The options are varied. They may decide that they have sufficient information, make a decision on the spot and inform the yachts accordingly. They may decide to take both skippers off their yachts and have a hearing on the water in an umpire boat, or they may decide that the only appropriate action is to wait until returning to the shore to open a full hearing. In this latter case, the hearing must be conducted as would a protest hearing under the normal rules.

These hearings, on- and off-the-water, are subject to requests for redress, reopening and appeals (appeals will not be available if an International Jury has been appointed). However the protest does not have to be in writing when initiated on-the-water and it is usual for the umpires to have addressed the validity of the protest on-the-water, even when continued ashore.

The other major change for match racing is that even if an infringement is found, the protest committee, which may include the umpires, has a choice of penalty when they decide that the infringement has not affected the outcome of the match. The options listed are:

- to impose a penalty of one point or part of one point

- to order a re-sail

- to make any other arrangement as deemed equitable, which may be to impose no penalty.

It is quite common in these circumstances for the penalty to be one-third of a point. This is sufficient to act as a tie breaker in a round robin series. These penalty options were included to reduce the incentive to lodge a 'technical protest' after losing a match. All the evidence is that it has been successful.

Protests against yachts in other matches

It is quite common for yachts to become involved with yachts in other matches. While it is quite rare for them to protest each other, the question is: if they do, should they use a Y flag or a B flag?

The appendix specifies that a Y flag is only used for a protest against 'the other yacht in her match' and so it is clear that the Y flag is not appropriate. This leads us towards using a 'B' flag, which would be quite logical were a match racing yacht to be involved with a racing, but not match racing yacht. (Can you imagine the surprise of yacht, not match racing, being chased by a high speed motor boat with people blowing whistles and waving flags at her!)

However, to allow a 'B' flag protest, without reservation, would be inconsistent with the principles of umpiring for those rules covered by Y flags between yachts in a match. Imagine that yacht Alpha witnesses an incident between yachts in another match (Bravo and Charlie), and that it may be in Alpha's best interest for one or other to win. Were she allowed to protest there would have to be a hearing after the race, exactly what umpiring is trying to avoid. As a consequence a yacht is only permitted to protest a yacht in another match when she alleges that she has been infringed against, or when alleging infringement of a rule outside the defined scope of on-the-water decisions by umpires.

The hearing could then address whether interfering with a yacht in another match was an issue, impossible if the Y flag were used. If it was decided that there was an infringement but the outcome of neither match was affected then the protest committee may use the flexibility of penalty provided by the appendix, detailed above.

Redress

The rule for seeking redress is rule 69. However, it is modified in one very important respect: 'A yacht requesting redress due to circumstances that arise prior to finishing shall display a protest flag at the first reasonable opportunity after she becomes aware of the circumstances that may justify her request, but not later than five minutes after finishing.'

Again, this is a modification intended to avoid a yacht that loses a match subsequently attempting unjustifiably to have the race ruled invalid, and consequently wasting everybody's time. It also gives the umpires the opportunity, on seeing the flag displayed, to look around for a reason why the flag might be flying.

There are some circumstances when redress is normally excluded by the sailing instructions; breakdowns after the first warning signal of a flight and interference by umpire boats are the two most common. Sometimes the latter is written to exclude the competitors from seeking redress but does not prohibit the umpires initiating a redress hearing themselves. Thus if the umpire boat really caused a major problem the race could be re-sailed, but if a little wash affected one of the yachts no action would be taken.

Para 8.2 from Appendix B6 says: 'No proceedings of any kind may be taken in relation to any action or non-action by the umpires when this appendix applies.'

This paragraph, implemented in 1992 onwards, means that whatever the umpires do or do not do on-the-water cannot be changed. We are moving ever closer to other sports and there is no doubt that these changes are, in part at least, for the benefit of the media. It used to be that if the umpires acted outside of their powers given by the appendix, then the competitors could claim redress (for example, a penalty being imposed on a yacht when her opponent had not protested). This is no longer the case. Umpires and competitors alike will have to get used to the new regime.

It is unclear if this also excludes the possibility of the umpires initiating, via the race committee, the abandonment of a race because 'the fairness of the competition has been affected' as allowed by rule 5.4(c)(iv) along similar lines to the following example.

Should there be an action or omission of the race committee that might materially prejudice the finishing position of a yacht this can be considered to affect the fairness of the competition and abandoned there and then. Take the case when the wrong recall signal is given, causing the wrong yacht, say Blue, to return, a clear case for redress. If the race is not abandoned then Yellow has to win this race in order for the race to be re-sailed. (If Blue should recover to win, there would be no prejudice to her finishing position). Having won once, Yellow will have to win again in order to score a point. While she was given an unfair advantage in the first place, it is still not equitable for her to have to win twice to score a point, but a re-sail is virtually the only redress that can be given in most match racing cases. Immediately abandoning the race also saves significant time, often a major bonus in what are normally very tightly scheduled events.

12

The management of match races

Consistent with the previous chapters of this book, when considering the management of match races we shall concentrate on those aspects that are peculiar to match racing. While primarily written for the race management team, these aspects should not be overlooked by competitors or umpires. Understanding what the race officials are trying to achieve, and some of the problems that they must resolve, goes a long way to eliminating frustration which can be so destructive to your own performance.

To some extent the development of match racing has suffered over the years because of its own high profile. Observers of the America's Cup and Grand Prix events see the massive organisations that are put in place and probably think that there is no way that they can put on a match racing event. All we can say is that if you went to the Olympics you would come away with the same impression about fleet racing. We hope you will see that match racing can be organised and managed perfectly satisfactorily with the minimum of resources.

As an example of the opposite extreme, John recalls a great day on-the-water. We took two J24s, each with a crew of four, down to the end of the Lymington River. One RIB followed with a crew of two, four coloured flags on sticks and a whistle. We were lucky enough to find two marks, about half a mile apart and almost perfectly in line upwind. We tied an anchor and line to a large fender and dropped it about eight boat lengths from the leeward of the two marks at almost right angles to the wind to form a starting/finishing line. The course was set: start, windward mark to starboard, leeward mark to starboard, windward mark to starboard, finish.

The yachts were assigned ends and a whistle was blown for the 10 minute attention signal. At 5 minutes there was another whistle and a Yellow flag was waved. The RIB took up station to leeward of the middle of the line. At 4 minutes there was another whistle and a Blue flag was waved. The yachts entered and the RIB became the umpire boat. At the start, there was another whistle with the RIB positioned as best it could to judge premature starters.

The race ran its course, with protests answered by either Green flag and whistle (no penalty) or Red flag, pointing finger and whistle (penalty for the yacht pointed at).

After each race came a change of personnel. Umpires became skippers, skippers became crew, crew became umpires, and so on until we ran out of time. You should have seen the joy on the face of a skipper, now an umpire, penalising the umpire now playing skipper!

From now on let's look at the middle ground between these two extremes.

First considerations

So, someone has decided that running a match racing event might be a good idea - perhaps simply to put some variety into the club programme, or as a competition between clubs (it doesn't matter). We will cover the various aspects in greater detail, but first you need to establish an overall plan for your event. You need to know who you are running the event for (that is, who will be the potential competitors), when you will run the event, and how much time it should take.

Who is going to run the event? What experience have they had? It may be that you are lucky enough to have someone who has had previous experience with match racing events, maybe as a competitor. If not it may well be worth while contacting someone with such experience, perhaps through another club, to act as an adviser - especially in the early stages. Match racing events generally become pretty hectic with a large number of races and all sorts of unfamiliar problems. It is also a good idea to appoint a 'race director' in addition to a principal race officer. The role of the race director is to handle organisational problems as they arise, thus allowing the principal race officer to get on with running the races.

It is also important at an early stage to identify the yachts that will be used and the level of budget that is available to run the event. Inevitably, the first match racing event run by a club tends to require some new equipment. This may range from as little as a few new flags to additional boats for mark laying and umpiring. (We have included, in the appendix, a detailed list of equipment required.)

The yachts

Are the crews going to supply their own yachts or are you, as the organisers, to provide the yachts? Sometimes each crew provides a yacht, but they are then all entered into a common draw. In this case the yachts should be considerd to be provided by the organising authority as far as Appendix B6 para 1.1, Damage, is concerned.

Obviously when the crews provide and sail their own yachts the workload and problems for the organisers are both significantly reduced. However, this approach will reduce the emphasis on match racing in favour of more conventional boatspeed, except in all but the strictest of one design fleets. If one or more yachts have new sails, perhaps they could be persuaded to put on older sets or indeed to make other modifications to equalise the boats.

Should you be in the fortunate position of being able to select the yachts you are going to use, it is best to choose those with a strong one-design record or those that are operated on a fleet basis. The newer the yachts and the nearer together in time they were built, the more consistent they are likely to be. From a fleet, pick out those with medium track records - avoid the best and the worst and, if necessary, do the same with the sails.

The time that the yachts are available before the event and the number of competent people at your disposal will determine the amount of work you can put into the yachts. This effort is directed at both equality and reliability. It is not possible to put a priority order on all the items that can be included in this preparation. It will depend upon what is possible and how large the differences are, but a list that includes most of the possibilities is included in Checklist 2, at the back of the book.

There is a general move towards lighter, higher performance yachts even for match racing. However, the few yachts that have been specifically designed and built for match racing on the Grand Prix circuit (where the organisers always provide the yachts) have avoided being too extreme. The rigs avoid the need for runners, for example.

Skippers and helmsmen

Who is entitled to enter? It is normal to limit this to 'invitees of the organising authority', but the number of entries needs to be worked out well in advance. If the event is to be a club event, it may be necessary to use a first come first served system to limit the numbers.

It is the skipper who is scored in match racing, not the yacht. Furthermore, the skippers often gain points that are used towards the IYRU ranking list for match racing skippers. The sailing instructions therefore restrict the helmsman to be the skipper, except in emergency.

Crew, crew numbers and weight

Having decided on the yachts and the skippers the next consideration is the crew - a term that always includes the helmsman/skipper. The question is how many are to crew each yacht and how heavy should they be? Crew numbers are usually established on the low side of a normal crew for the yachts. However, this depends upon the objectives of the event, which may be to involve as many people as possible. The common weight limit is an average of 187 lb (85 kg) per crew member when dressed in at least shorts and shirts. Stipulating a weight limit means that you will need a set of scales available as the crews register. It is also important to have some check weights available as there are always arguments about the accuracy of the scales! One of the best sources of such weights is the local gymnasium.

Event format

To discuss event format, we first need to clarify some match racing terminology. A *match* is a race between two yachts. A *flight* is a number of matches in one scheduled starting sequence. A *series* is a number of matches to determine which skipper shall progress to the next round, or win the event. A *round robin series* is a series of matches in which each skipper sails once against each other skipper. A *knock out series* is a series of races between two skippers only. A *group* is a part of the total entry.

There are many possible formats for a match racing event. The America's Cup, as distinct from the challenger and defender selection series, has been a 'first to win four races' knock out series. The phrase 'first to win four races' is a phrase used in preference to 'best of seven' just in case one of the matches is tied for any reason. (This happened in the Louis Vuitton Cup 1992 when the jury penalised New Zealand by taking a win away without awarding the match to Il Moro de Venezia.)

When the Grand Prix events first started they were entirely single round robins. As the publicity surrounding these events increased, the demand for semi finals and finals grew in order to give the events a climax. Gradually the circuit has moved to shorter races and this has given the opportunity to introduce two round robins. The 'standard' number of entries is ten. There is one notable exception: the Omega Gold Cup held in Bermuda. This event invites eight 'seeded' skippers who pay no entry fee and there are places for an additional sixteen fee-paying entries. The fee is considerable, being in excess of $1,000. These sixteen entries are divided into two *groups* of eight, each of which sail a round robin. The top four from each group go forward to meet a seeded skipper and from now on the competition is entirely knock out. It is very popular with the competitors (except for the seeds who get knocked out in the first round!) and provides one of the few opportunities for new blood to enter top-level match racing. Prize money is structured such that if you get through the first knock out round you cover at least your entry fee.

Yet another alternative is that adopted for the British National Championships and is designed to give the maximum possible number of crews an opportunity to enter. Each regional heat and the championship itself are scheduled for a two day weekend. Up to eighteen crews are accepted for each heat and the event has six yachts available. The eighteen are divided into three groups of six, who each sail a round robin (five races per crew).

Rather than sail each group straight off they will sail either two or three races before handing the yachts over to another group. This gives the crews some thinking time to account for what may have been their first attempt at match racing.

The winner of each group goes through to a semi final. The second and third from each group make up a new group of six. This group sail a final round robin and the winner takes the fourth semi final slot. Semi finals and finals (first to win two races) brings each event to a conclusion.

The range of possibilities is considerable. In order to select the most appropriate for your event, you need some more information relating to the time available and how long it takes to run the various formats. We move on to that next, but before we do, remember that you will need to build in some contingency plans for when the weather or breakdowns do not allow you to complete the programme as planned.

Event schedules

Match racing events are being held in more and more confined waters. The main reason for this has been to increase the availability of the action on-the-water to spectators, but a spin-off benefit is that the course area is frequently much nearer the yacht club or marina acting as the event base. The time required at each end of the day is reduced and the time available for racing can be increased significantly. Allow for a morning briefing each day. The first will take the best part of an hour, but on subsequent days twenty minutes should be enough. The crews can be rigging the boats while the briefing is in progress if any draw for yachts is done first. Sometimes the draw is carried out beforehand and the results put in sealed envelopes in order to save time.

The time it takes to set up the course should give the crews sufficient time to get used to the conditions and be ready to start.

Each race should be scheduled for a racing time between 20 and 30 minutes, no more. Given the starting sequence from Appendix B6 the entire race should take 40 minutes plus 5 minutes for each additional pair. In practice, an hour per flight is a good working number. There is no need for a lunch break, provided that food has been put on board beforehand. The nature of the system is that each yacht will get an extended period between some matches. The race committee and umpires have to take advantage of lulls in the action.

From the above you should be able to work out the racing time available to you and thus how many flights you can attempt. Given the number of yachts and crew involved, a suitable format can be developed, including, as we have said before, a contingency plan.

Advertising

As a greater percentage of match racing events seek sponsorship which in turn leads to advertising, it is appropriate to mention the subject here - not in the sense of how to attract sponsorship but how to handle the advertising issues.

The advertising category will need to be stated in the notice of race together with any requirements for competitors to display adverts on their clothing or yachts. It is also wise to require any crew wishing to display personal adverts of any kind to have such adverts approved beforehand and to state that, when in conflict with the event sponsors, they may be disallowed. When the organising authority provide the yachts, the extent to which the yachts will be available for personal advertising should be included.

Should you be in the fortunate position of having television interest or even be considering producing a video, do talk to the television company first about what is and what is not permitted by their regulations. For instance, under IYRR category B, advertising on clothing can be on the front or the back. Under some countries' regulations, advertising on the back of a competitor will be edited out from any transmitted material.

The notice of race

We have now discussed the items that are required to be included in the notice of race. Rule 2 of the IYRR, which should always be used as a guide, includes a list of these and also optional items that should be included when appropriate.

We include in Checklist 3 at the back of the book a list of items for the notice of race that might not be obvious from IYRR rule 2.

The course

The vast majority of match races are based on windward and leeward legs only. It has become standard to locate the starting line to leeward of all the rounding marks and to use the same line as the finishing line, thus creating downwind finishes.

Fig 144 shows the most common course. This has a number of advantages. Using the same line for starting and finishing not only reduces the number of committee boats required, but also keeps to a minimum the time between flights for the yachts to reassemble. Having the line to leeward keeps the yachts not racing, and spectators, out of the way of those fighting it out on the race course. From the race officer's point of view he can see the whole course and all the action without having to look over his shoulder. However, it must be said that when the line used to be set in the middle of the beat, the committee boat was never far from the action either.

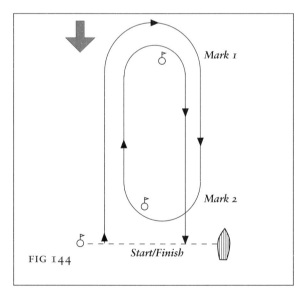

FIG 144

Mark 1

Mark 2

Start/Finish

The marks are shown as being rounded to starboard, again becoming standard. At the windward mark there is a slight advantage to the yacht behind but most importantly it opens up the options on the run. The left-hand side is favoured in order to approach the mark on starboard tack, but the right hand side is favoured for the inside berth.

The number of rounds is normally two, making the course: start, mark 1, mark 2, mark 1, finish. In order for the race to be set at about 25 minutes, the first beat should take 7 to 8 minutes in the absence of current. Fig 145 shows that at 4 knots VMG, for example, the windward leg (start to mark 1) should be 0.5 nautical miles. If the course area will not permit legs of even this length then more rounds will have to be set.

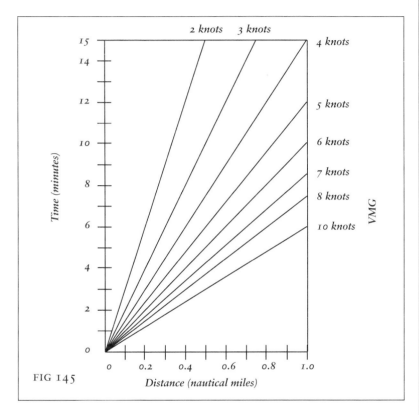

FIG 145

In Fig 144 we saw that mark 2 is set to windward of the starting line. Bearing in mind that there will be some pairs of yachts on the course when others are just starting, it is important to keep this mark a reasonable distance - about 100 yds (90 m), upwind of the line. If the distances chosen result in one pair rounding the mark just as another pair pass the mark having just started, then change the distances for the next flight (unless the windspeed changes). Some confusion between matches at some time is inevitable, but the race committee should work to minimise the problem.

The perennial problem for a race officer trying to set a course is a wind that will just not settle down, especially as the pressure of trying to complete all the scheduled races grows. In one sense match racing events are more difficult. Unless you get to the final and sail at least one match, it can be impossible to find a fair winner. On the other hand, some shifting of the wind after the start is not the same problem as it is with a big fleet. In the big fleet race, even a moderate shift in the wind will give a large advantage to those on the favoured side. In match racing, accounting for possible shifts either left or right is very much an intrinsic skill of the game and this gives the race officer some freedom when setting the windward mark. Not that this should be done carelessly, but it is quite reasonable to monitor the wind direction and set the mark at the mean. Swings of 15 degrees either side should not cause concern and sometimes, when you know that it is not going to improve, you have to settle for worse than that.

One other consideration when setting the marks, and the windward mark in particular, is the proximity of local features that affect the wind. As we have already stated, it is not the windshifts that are a problem, as competitors can plan and sail to account for these. The problem occurs when the windward mark is set just on the edge of the breeze as it hits the water. Sometimes it will blow, allowing a yacht to round the mark and set off down the run with pace; at other times the wind will die and so does the chance of the yacht winning the race. This is pure luck that no amount of skill can overcome, and yet can often be avoided by moving the mark as little as a couple of boat lengths.

Starting and finishing lines

For the same reasons as for the windward mark position, the bias on a match race starting line is not so critical as with fleet racing. It is best not deliberately to set any bias, as the wind will normally create some for you anyway. It is up to the match racing crew to beat their opponent in any given set of circumstances and that includes assessing and using any favoured end of the starting line.

The length of the starting line is critical, as it determines the size of the safe triangle described back in Chapter 2. This in turn has a major impact on the pre-start manoeuvres and tactics available. If the line is too long, the yachts will not have to fight for position; the line bias becomes more important; and it becomes too difficult to trap an opponent. If it is too short, the safe triangle becomes so small that there is not enough safe area for both yachts. One will then win the start by a large margin and the opportunity for an interesting match will be lost. The best guide is that it should take the yachts between 30 and 40 seconds to sail the length of the line. In moderate conditions this is equivalent to about 8 boat lengths.

The final consideration is the location of the starting line, which can be a problem when moving events into less open waters. In order to allow the yachts proper opportunity to manoeuvre, there should be an absolute minimum of 50 yards of clear water to leeward of the line and for the same distance along the layline approaches. Particularly important is the avoidance of underwater obstructions in this area, and ideally even spectators should be kept out of this area.

When using the committee boat as one end of the starting line, it should be at the starboard end. This gives a slight disadvantage to the yacht entering from this end as she will have to sail deeper and more slowly to cross the line as required by Appendix B6 (para 4.2). This acts as a balance to her advantage of being the right of way yacht. While it is obviously essential that the committee boat is well anchored, an over long anchor line increases the problems for the starboard end yacht. Should this be unavoidable, then the starting line itself should be lengthened by a similar amount. A marker buoy attached to the anchor line at keel depth seems to avoid the problems of fouling, both when entering and off the starting line.

With a buoy at one end and a vessel at the other, the two ends of the line will probably be anchored on different cable lengths. Any change in current that affects the lie of these will have a relatively large effect on such short starting lines. Again, this may justify a slightly longer starting line.

The starting line eventually becomes the finishing line. It is often a matter of sheer practicality that the marks are not moved. With five pairs on the course the last pair will start only minutes before the first pair finish.

Spectators

When setting up the course consideration should be given to any spectators or spectator fleet that are expected. Provided that they are anchored, spectator vessels can be surprisingly close to the action without an adverse effect on the racing. Indeed, in the pre-start period they offer opportunities to increase the tactical options, but should remain outside the laylines at either end or well to leeward of the starting line.

There are three ways to 'control' spectators on-the-water, and frequently it is necessary to use all three:

■ On official spectator boats it is best to provide an on board person to guide the skipper. This person can often provide some form of commentary for those on board.

■ Small runabouts to act as marshalls can be effective provided that they are well identified.

■ The proper use of marine band VHF radio will work once it becomes known which channel will provide race information.

Cross current

With a current of any magnitude across the course, it becomes impossible to set a reasonable beat and a run using only two marks. Of the two, it is more important that the run is true as long as the windward leg remains a beat, but eventually a wing mark has to be used to set a reaching leg from the windward mark into the current. This means that the direction of current determines the side on which the marks are to be rounded. Looking upwind, with a current from left to right, set the marks to port and vice versa. The reaching leg is usually set near right angles to the windward leg and the sailing instructions will prohibit the use of spinnakers until rounding to wing mark in order to avoid damage.

The length of the reach is a function of the cross course component of the current, the VMG of the yachts downwind, and the length of the downwind leg.

Shortening, postponing and abandoning

A good rule to follow is that you never shorten a match race. It is, however, acceptable to use the shorten course flag before the start to signal that a short course (start, mark 1, finish) will be used. Should your programme be running short of time, this is a better solution than trying to work out a result when the round robin has not been completed for instance. We think that this is also better than drawing lots to break ties.

When using the course as in Fig 144 the best way to set a shorter course is to move mark 2 up towards the windward mark 1. This shortens the overall course, retains a respectable first beat and last run, while establishing an interesting boat handling, mark rounding section in the middle. It also clears the leeward mark from the immediate vicinity of the start.

Postponing a whole flight is really no different to any other form of racing except that, as we have said, there is no need to do so for marginal windshifts. Sometimes, though, there is no option but to postpone some starts part way through a start sequence - when the first leg is no longer a beat, for instance. This again is really no different from a postponement in the middle of a multi-class start sequence.

Abandoning a match race in progress is a very contentious issue, similar to shortening, unless the reason is to rectify some obvious error by race committee or umpires that has affected the fairness of the competition. To abandon a match because of a windshift, even a massive one, can be very unfair. Suppose in the pre-start you managed to manoeuvre your opponent into a couple of penalties such that even before the first mark you had a very substantial lead. Is it fair to abandon such a race whatever the windshift? On the other hand, the match racing penalties were designed such that the penalised yacht would stand some chance of winning and those chances are severely reduced if there is no beat or square run. Over all it seems to be about right that the first leg should be a beat and that, providing it is, then the match should be left to run its course. If this policy is adopted, it is best declared at the briefing and then put into practice in order to eliminate claims for redress.

To abandon an individual match, the N should be flown over the numeral pendant or whatever signal is used for the warning signal of the match concerned. The umpires should be informed by radio and they can verbally draw the yachts' attention to the signal in order to get them back ready to re-start as soon as possible.

Recalls

One advantage of match racing is that the race committee do not need the first substitute flag, there are no general recalls. Should there be an error in the starting sequence any thus affected match that has already started can be abandoned.

Individual recalls though are frequent, and require smart work on the committee boat. By far the best system is when the Blue/Yellow system of yacht identification is used. The line spotter should have these flags on sticks, one in each hand. In this way the recall can be visually signalled with the minimum of delay while the gunner responds immediately to the hail of 'Recall'. Three seconds' delay for a recall signal is unacceptable for match racing and may well result in the umpires requesting the match be abandoned for immediate re-sail. This means that it must be the line spotter who lifts the flags.

Smart sailing instructions will allow the recall flag to be lowered after 1 minute even if the yacht has not responded. This will coincide with the preparatory signal for the next start.

Time limits

To some extent time limits for a match race only serve the purpose of ensuring that a reasonable average speed is maintained - otherwise, the match will be abandoned. However they do carry a great risk. Suppose that on the last day of your event the wind is dying and the time limit runs out on the final, just as the yachts approach the finishing line. If time limits are set, they have to be so long as to be virtually useless when so many races are scheduled. It is far better to use a race committee who understand what is likely to happen, and set a suitably short course and forget time limits as such.

It is quite common, though, to include a sailing instruction to the effect that in any match a yacht finishing 5 minutes after her opponent is deemed to have retired. This has no effect on the scoring as there are no points for second place, and it does ensure that there is a limit on the hold-up in proceedings when waiting for one particular yacht to finish.

Changing course

Changing the course in mid race is quite difficult and the more pairs that are on the course the more difficult it becomes. In practice, only the windward mark ever gets changed and there are arguments that in such short races they should either be abandoned or allowed to run as set. On the other hand, we have seen occasions when such changes have saved the day. What is needed is:

- very distinctive change marks
- well briefed mark laying crews
- a large code flag C, and
- a good sound source that can get close to the mark without interfering with the races.

Committee boats

As we saw at the beginning of this chapter, a RIB on the move with one 'race officer' and one driver can do the job. Realistically, though, an absolute minimum of three people are required for an event. One timekeeper/sound signaller, one flag signaller (much easier with flags on sticks rather than halyards), and a race officer who calls the line and, as we have seen, displays the recall flags if required. If you have more people available all well and good, as there is plenty to do. It goes without saying that the committee vessel is normally a compromise between what you would like and what is available. It needs to be large enough for the personnel on board and suitable for the conditions you can expect on the race course.

It is worth taking some time to work out how all the possible signals will be displayed without obstructing one another. The use of number and letter boards, for information that can be displayed early and normally remains displayed for at least the duration of a flight starting sequence, can relieve possible flag congestion and make life easier for all concerned.

If you intend to use firearms and cartridges, do add up all the signals you are going to have to make sure you have sufficient.

While audible sound signals are very important, the small distances involved do not always require cartridges. It is worth considering using them only for the attention signal and the first warning signal of each flight, which is when the yachts are likely to be furthest away.

In addition to the committee boat, you will need at least one mark layer - two are better. These can double up as umpire boats once the course is laid. As soon as the first match in a flight has finished, that umpire boat should stand by to move the windward mark as soon as the last pair are round, ready for the next flight. This saves personnel and boats, but does limit the option to change the course during a flight and can be inconvenient if protest hearings are required between flights.

Starting sequences

After a period of evolution the starting sequence in Appendix B6 para 3 has met with universal acceptance (with the sole exception of the America's Cup). It is worth noting that there are a lot of signals and the time intervals are varied. The timekeeper has to be someone with the ability to concentrate and not be distracted by the action going on around them.

There is an area of direct interaction with the umpires. This is in relation to para 4.2 of Appendix B6 which reads: 'Within the two-minute period following her preparatory signal, a yacht shall first cross and clear the starting line from the course side to the pre-start side'. The 2 minute signal in the starting sequence is omitted if both yachts have complied with para 4.2.

First, this requires that someone on the committee boat is continually watching both yachts from their 4 minute preparatory signal onwards. When they have observed both yachts cross and clear the starting line (all of the yacht, its crew and equipment must completely clear the starting line) from the course side, a message needs to get to the gunner that no sound signal is required. Should either yacht first cross the line from the pre-course side then whatever happens subsequently they do not comply, it is not possible to 'unwind' the error as you can when rounding a mark the wrong way. When either yacht fails to meet the requirement, then the signal must be given and the umpires informed which yacht has infringed. The umpires then impose a penalty on the appropriate yacht. If there is any doubt which yacht infringed and radios are not available, the umpires will have to close the committee boat on hearing the sound signal to receive the information verbally.

Should one yacht break down it is often best to postpone the particular match and get on with the rest of the flight. When doing this it is most usual to leave the appropriate start blank and leave the starting times of the subsequent matches as they were. Often it is possible to add the affected pair on to the back end of the sequence, thus losing only five minutes. If the match cannot be started at this time it is best to leave it to the end of the round robins altogether, for it may not need to be sailed. This approach is also wise when the protest committee order a match to be re-sailed. Whatever the race committee decide to do in these circumstances, they should inform the umpires who in turn can verbally let the intentions of the race committee be known to the yachts in the pair that they will umpire.

Round robins

Round robins require pairing lists in order to decide who sails who, when, and to which end of the starting line each is assigned. Pairing lists for six, eight and ten skipper round robins are shown in Checklist 4. These have been worked out to ensure that:

- each skipper sails each other
- each has a fair share of port end starts (they cannot be exactly the same with an odd number of flights)
- no skipper has too many consecutive starts from the same end
- no skipper starts in match 1 having just sailed the last match of the previous flight
- as far as is possible each skipper has a balanced set of starts throughout the sequence (match 1, 2, 3 etc)

There are two ways of allocating the skippers a number for the purposes of the pairing lists. Either they can be drawn or they can be allocated. If they are allocated, it means that the programme can be published well in advance; this helps everyone understand what is going on. The pairing lists are also constructed such that if the skippers are ranked and the numbers allocated on the basis of the ranking, then the most evenly matched skippers race in the last flight, hopefully creating a more exciting climax.

If two round robins are sailed, the numbers could be re-allocated based on the positions at the end of the first round robin, but it is more usual simply to use the same pairing list, reversing port and starboard throughout. Again this can be published in advance and saves issuing a new list part way through a day on-the-water. (You never finish a complete round robin at the end of a day - Murphy's Law of match race management.)

Semi finals and finals

The semi finals are usually the first to win a minimum of two races, and in some events up to the first to win four. The two winning semi finalists go through to the 1st and 2nd place final, while the losers sail off for 3rd and 4th places. The 3rd/4th place final should be scheduled for fewer races than the 1st/2nd final in an attempt to ensure the latter is the last race on-the-water.

The draw and assigned ends for these races will often need to be completed on-the-water. It is quite acceptable for the race committee to make the draw and the results can be quickly copied and delivered to each yacht by the umpires. The sailing instructions do need to make provision for such changes.

The draw for assigned ends only needs to cover the first match in the series. For following matches, the ends are alternated.

Organisers providing the yachts

When the organising authority provides the boats additional instructions are required to specify how the boats are to be allocated and what will happen in the event of breakdown. The redress rule is usually modified so that breakdowns after the first warning signal of each flight do not give grounds for redress unless caused by a yacht that was required to keep clear.

Will the class rules apply? If the class rules are applied and one competitor happens to have been provided with a boat that is out of class, this is not much of a problem (except the issue of equality of the yachts). Should a protest be lodged and upheld, providing it was 'no fault of her own' (that is the crew had done nothing to put the boat out of class), she would be entitled to redress for the action of the race committee in providing her with a boat out of class.

However, there are often other 'funnies' (modification to rule 54, Propulsion, for instance) in class rules that competitors may unwittingly infringe - or, just as importantly, might not know to take advantage of. Organisers would not wish to provide each entrant with a set of class rules for easy night time reading! It is best therefore not to include the class rules in the rules of the regatta, but to substitute 'rules for inspection', as they have become known. Essentially these forbid any modification to the boat and ensure that they are sailed in a manner unlikely to cause damage.

Briefings and communications

Unlike fleet racing, which moves as far away from giving verbal information at briefings as possible, most match racing regattas have daily morning briefings. There are nearly always some questions relating to the yachts that need to be resolved and it is a convenient opportunity to hand out sailing instruction amendments. Any questions the skippers have relating to the yachts are normally submitted in writing in such a way that they can be answered with a simple 'yes' or 'no'. The answer can be written on the paper and the whole question then posted on the official notice board for all to see.

A wise organising committee also makes provision for amendments to sailing instructions to be issued while afloat. They may only be used for things like the pairing list and assigned ends for the next round to be issued, but without the facility progress can sometimes be very difficult.

Sail combinations

Match racing is not intended to be between yachts with different foresails and different numbers of reefs in the mainsails. The race committee control the sail plan to be used at any one time and generally err on the side of small sails. This ensures that the emphasis is maintained on match racing skills.

Sailing instructions

Having worked all of this out and how it is to be put into practice, the sailing instructions can now be written.

The sailing instructions for match racing vary in size from a few pages to over twenty. When umpiring was first used there was no Appendix B6, and so all that is contained in the appendix had to appear as sailing instructions. The appendix remains in a state of change, reviewed on an annual basis. As problems are discovered, they are first tackled and tested in sailing instructions and the good ones become part of the next revision of the appendix. Fortunately, we are now through the period of major changes and so the sailing instructions are tending to reduce in size.

We have included a list of the topics to be covered by the sailing instructions in Checklist 5 as a useful guide and we wish you enjoyable match race management.

Checklist 1
Equipment

This appendix lists the requirements for match racing and gives a checklist for competitors, umpires, judges and race committees. The specification for each item (e g flags) will depend on the type of yachts and the event being sailed but in general flags are made too small. Obviously, they are no use if you cannot see them, so some guidance is given here in addition to the details in Chapter 3.

Yachts

Protest flag - code flag Y: 300 mm x 400 mm on 1 m stick
Protest flag - code flag B: 200 mm x 300 mm with lanyards
Breakdown flag - code flag L: 300 mm x 400 mm with lanyards
               - or white

Identification flags - one blue: 500 mm x 650 mm on stick
                             one yellow: 500 mm x 650 mm on stick

Committee boat

In addition to the normal complete set of code flags:

Identification flags - one blue: 800 mm x 1000 mm on stick
(for recalls)   one yellow: 800 mm x 1000 mm on stick

Radio - VHF with umpire channel plus own working channel.

Sound signals - Guns and horns, or two types of horn if possible.

Umpire boats and wing boats

In all but very rough water, umpire and wing boats should be 5 - 6 m rigid inflatables, dories or whalers, with a minimum of 60 hp. In rough waters they should be 6 - 8 m sports boats with adequate spray protection.

They must have all-round visibility and handholds as umpires frequently work standing up. Steering equipment and controls must be in good order and the boats must have adequate fuel capacity for a full day's work.

Umpire boat signals:

No penalty - Green flag: 800 mm x 1000 mm on stick 1000 mm long
Penalty -   Blue: 800 mm x 1000 mm on stick 1000 mm long
             Yellow: 800 mm x 1000 mm on stick 1000 mm long
DSQ -   Black: 800 mm x 1000 mm on stick 1000 mm long

Identification: White flag with red or black 'Umpire'
                800 mm x 1000 mm mounted behind the umpires

Radio - Marine VHF, waterproof. Preferable to have one channel per match capability in addition to race committee.

General - Adhesive tape and thin line.

Umpires and wing judges

Each umpire needs the following, which they should provide themselves unless marked *:

Sound source - referee's whistle

Sailing instructions/notice of race *

Schedule of races on waterproof card *

Life jackets if local regulations require *

Uniforms as required by organisers *

Note book, preferably wet notes with pencil

Tape recorder

Observers

Each observer needs the following:

Jacket, lightweight to go over own clothing. Half of them Blue and half of them Yellow can be 'athletes number vest' type.

Water bottles or other weight that they can take onto the yachts and attach to the stern to equalise the pairs.

Checklist 2
Equalisation of
the yachts

Hull and appendages

Weight
Underwater surfaces - similar and clean
Equally stripped out
Same rudders and keels
Maximum rudder angle
Propellers - size and type

Rig and rigging

Mast position and rake
Black bands or sail extreme positions
Gooseneck position
Standing rigging - lengths and tensions
Spreaders - length and angles
Halyards - number, material, length, tensioning and cleating, sail
    attachments, stoppers
Spinnaker pole height on mast

Sails

Size, condition, cloth weight, material
Reefing points and reefing system
Cunningham hole position
Headboard
Cringle positions
Fairlead positions, control systems and movement range
Batten lengths and stiffness
Boltrope type and size

Equipment

Vang - type, purchase, line length, cleating
Lifeline tension
Spinnaker pole length, fittings, weight, bridle
Headsail feeder
Toolkits
Spare ropes, mooring lines and fenders
Compasses
Anchors and line - weight, type and position for stowage
Tiller length, extension type and length
Control line arrangements and cleating
Instruments - wind direction indicators, etc
Radios
Number and type of winch handles
Hiking aids
Water and fuel tanks - equally full (fuel), empty (water)

Checklist 3
Notice of race contents

(See also IYRR 2, Notice of Race.)

- Appendix B6 (year) to be included in rules governing the regatta.

- If the system of umpiring is not to be used?

- Eligibility of skippers.

- Crew numbers per yacht and any weight limit including the time when weighing is to take place.

- The approximate course area.

- The yachts to be used.

- The intended event format and schedule.

- The advertising Category (although listed in IYRR rule 2 we highlight this item here for emphasis).

- Damage deposits.

Checklist 4
Pairing lists
for round robins

4 yachts

Flight	1	2	3
Match 1	1 v 2	4 v 2	1 v 4
Match 2	3 v 4	3 v 1	2 v 3

6 yachts

Flight	1	2	3	4	5
Match 1	4 v 5	3 v 5	3 v 2	6 v 3	6 v 5
Match 2	1 v 3	2 v 4	4 v 6	5 v 2	2 v 1
Match 3	2 v 6	6 v 1	5 v 1	1 v 4	4 v 3

8 yachts

Flight	1	2	3	4	5
Match 1	6 v 3	6 v 4	5 v 2	1 v 5	4 v 1
Match 2	4 v 5	2 v 8	3 v 8	7 v 3	6 v 7
Match 3	7 v 2	5 v 3	1 v 6	8 v 4	5 v 8
Match 4	8 v 1	7 v 1	4 v 7	2 v 6	3 v 2

Flight	6	7
Match 1	7 v 5	8 v 7
Match 2	8 v 6	1 v 2
Match 3	2 v 4	3 v 4
Match 4	1 v 3	6 v 5

10 yachts

Flight	1	2	3	4	5
Match 1	1 v 3	10 v 8	9 v 4	2 v 5	3 v 9
Match 2	10 v 2	6 v 9	8 v 2	7 v 3	10 v 1
Match 3	9 v 8	4 v 7	3 v 5	1 v 9	4 v 8
Match 4	7 v 6	2 v 3	1 v 7	10 v 4	6 v 2
Match 5	5 v 4	5 v 1	6 v 10	8 v 6	5 v 7

Flight	6	7	8	9
Match 1	1 v 8	2 v 4	7 v 10	6 v 5
Match 2	4 v 6	7 v 9	5 v 8	4 v 3
Match 3	2 v 7	10 v 5	3 v 6	2 v 1
Match 4	9 v 5	8 v 3	1 v 4	9 v 10
Match 5	3 v 10	6 v 1	9 v 2	8 v 7

In each case the yacht on the left hand side is assigned the port end of the starting line. Should a double round robin be sailed all the pairings should be reversed for the second round.

Checklist 5
Sailing instructions: contents

See also IYRR rule 3.2

Rules applicable

Eligibility

Communications with competitors - notices and briefings

Changes to sailing instructions (procedure for)

Yachts and sails

Identification and assignment of the yachts

Crews, crew numbers and weight

Schedule of races for each round

Racing days

Premature termination of the event

Racing area and course

Marks

Breakdown procedures

Starting line and procedure

Finishing line

Changing the course during racing

Scoring

Any variation to Appendix B6 penalties

Haul out and cleaning restrictions

Advertising

Television cameras

Prizes and prizegiving

Index

Note: def. signifys definition of term.